Apologizing for God

Apologizing for God

The Importance of Living in History

MARK S. McLEOD-HARRISON

CASCADE Books • Eugene, Oregon

APOLOGIZING FOR GOD
The Importance of Living in History

Copyright © 2011 Mark S. McLeod-Harrison. All rights reserved. Except for brief quotations in critical publications or reviews, no part of this book may be reproduced in any manner without prior written permission from the publisher. Write: Permissions, Wipf and Stock Publishers, 199 W. 8th Ave., Suite 3, Eugene, OR 97401.

Cascade Books
An Imprint of Wipf and Stock Publishers
199 W. 8th Ave., Suite 3
Eugene, OR 97401

www.wipfandstock.com

ISBN 13: 978-1-60899-766-4

Cataloging-in-Publication data:

McLeod-Harrison, Mark S.

    Apologizing for God : the importance of living in history / Mark S. McLeod-Harrison.

    xiv + 152 p. ; 23 cm. — Includes bibliographical references.

    ISBN 13: 978-1-60899-766-4

    1. Philosophical theology. 2. Christianity—Philosophy. I. Title.

BT40 .M425 2011

Manufactured in the U.S.A.

*For my two sons,
Micah and Ian.*

*Go with God,
and make some history.*

Contents

Preface | ix
Introduction | xiii

1. Story | 1
2. Fiction | 7
3. Naming | 16
4. History | 24
5. Freewill | 32
6. Persons | 45
7. Heresy | 53
8. Hope | 58
9. Death | 63
10. Miracle | 71
11. Reason | 75
12. Faith | 79
13. Sacrament | 84
14. Virtue | 91
15. Work | 96
16. Suffering | 99
17. Reality | 107
18. Voice | 112
19. Sexism | 119
20. Community | 132
21. Time | 137

Appendix: *Words and the World* | 143
Bibliography | 151

Preface

ONE SHOULDN'T, IN ONE sense, have to apologize for God. In fact, such an apology would certainly be presumptuous. Yet often I feel it wouldn't be a bad idea for the divinity to apologize. Some of the things God does, or at least apparently so, certainly appear to need apologies, and deep ones at that. Yet God talks a whole lot less than I would wish. In this sense, I'll leave the apologies to God.

In another sense, apology is in order. Plato's *Apology* presents Socrates' defense against at least two charges: atheism and corruption of the youth. As it turns out, I've been accused, or so it would seem, of both—but more on that below. Since what I've just said about me seems to put me in pretty good company (after all, beside Jesus, who's had more influence in Western culture than Socrates?), perhaps I need to explain a little. What follows here falls far short of the power of Plato's reconstructed account of Socrates' day in court, where his last truly public speech and discourse is so marvelously expressed. Yet what I've written mirrors Socrates' apology in some ways. He defended himself by appealing to God. I will defend God by appealing to myself.

Did I just write that? Yes. Let me quickly clarify. I'm not writing to say I'm sorry in the stead of God. Rather I'm writing to show the plausibility of God's being from my own life. That's better. Maybe. Still pretty arrogant. Who am I to defend God's being on the basis of my own biography? So let's say it's not just me. Instead I have a good many friends who join with me, and from whom I have learned a great deal. I am not ashamed to recognize that I borrow heavily from some of the giants of the past, particularly those from whom I've learned the most philosophically and culturally.

I write about God by identifying where two extremes in our culture go astray, or lead us astray. I propose that by living between the extremes we find ourselves in history, walking with God. That makes the book partially about me. But this book is a philosophical work, although not, for the most part, a rigorous bit of philosophy. Often I just state my beliefs rather than provide my reasons. Nor is this truly autobiography. I don't think my life will be all that interesting to others, even though I am rather partial toward it. And the book certainly is not the standard sort of apology for God's existence or a standard sort of apology for Christianity, the religion that happens to be my home. Instead there are some stories, some theory, some guesswork, and some general poking around the edges of some important issues. Some chapters are more theoretical than others, but even in the theoretical ones I use a lot of metaphor and analogy to communicate, rather than detailed academic analysis. In that way, the book is more like a sketch than a completed painting. Some chapters are, however, full of stories of my life or they are bits of observation book-ended by stories. I try to explain why in the first chapter, but in a way, the whole book should help the appearance of arrogance in putting forth my life as a defense for God. It is not about me, in the end, but about us, together.

There's a good bit of theology in these pages as well, alongside the philosophy. As a Christian writing, thinking, and talking about philosophy, I cannot, nor do I believe I should, disassociate my philosophical positions from my theological ones. Again, some chapters are more theological or religious than others but for the most part I hope there is the kind of unity of thought and life that is appropriate for someone who has thought about how to be a Christian—and tried to live as a Christian—for some time. There are failures, of course. I'm nowhere near sainthood. If there is a purgatory, I expect to spend some time there getting things right.

After chapter 1, the first several chapters are the most theoretical. The appendix, too, relies on some more specialized background knowledge that some readers will have, although it can still be read, I hope, for profit. Chapter 1 introduces the work. Chapters 2 through 5 provide the general framework for the essay but can be summarized by saying that we don't make up the (whole) of reality but that history (a certain sort of objectivity) embroiders how we must live, and yet we are free and therefore can change and make not only the future but the actual way(s) the world is. After that, the chapters become somewhat more standalone and could, for the most part, be read as individual essays, in a variety of orders. Still, I've laid the book out the way I have because one thought led to another as I was writing. The last few chapters are more autobiographical, yet each one has an important point to make. Some of these points overlap with ones made earlier in the text, while others are new or, in a sense, applications of what I say elsewhere.

The main thesis I present is that we ought to reject the more radical forms of postmodernism we find in our culture. On the other hand, I think we ought to reject the older but no less disturbing modernism as well. I use the nature of fiction as an extended metaphor for what I take to be wrong with radical postmodernism. I use history as an extended but more grounded metaphor for a middle position between radical postmodernism and modernism. I propose that we live in history. Although history is in some ways fixed, living history opens out to the possibilities of the future in freedom and hope.

By "radical postmodernism" I mean the denial that there is anything true independent of human perspectives (frameworks, worldviews, conceptual schemes, or what have you). By "modernism" I mean the strict realist or objectivist view that proposes that what is true is more or less totally independent of human perspectives. My own view is in between these two. A good deal of what is true depends in important ways on humans and our perspectives. (In my case, technically, what is true depends on our conceptual schemes. But I won't be entering that technical and complex discussion here.) But we cannot make the ways the world is all alone, without falling into the total relativism of the radically postmodern. God provides the final truth and framework about the universe and the various and competing ways it is. God works with us *in history*, however, to construct the ways the world is. I propose, thus, a moderate sort of postmodernism—what I elsewhere call "theistic ontological pluralism."[1] But that's the last time you'll hear that technical phrase, for I'm not writing here for so-called "professional" philosophers but for everyone.

So in this book, I try to avoid as much technical language as I'm able and to communicate what I think about God and the world in something closer to a "lay" person's terms. I try to explain my view and truly "apologize" for God in language non-specialists can grasp. Chapters 2 through 5 may be a little uphill for some readers. Beyond chapters 2 through 5

1. See McLeod-Harrison, *Make/believing the World(s)*.

—and even there for many folks—I think most folk will face no special challenges. Some ideas are worth working at, however, and I hope what I have to say is clear and accessible enough to be worth the effort.

Introduction

G. K. Chesterton says of his book *Orthodoxy* that "it is unavoidably affirmative and therefore unavoidably autobiographical."[1] This essay is also unavoidably affirmative, at least for the most part. I'm not saying Christianity is the only plausible way to live in the world. I am saying it is one way, and a good one. Further, while I'm certainly not trying to say that my understanding of Christianity is the only way, I am suggesting that belief in God is the right way to think about the world. Theism is what I hold and, in fact, the Christian version of it. But bare theism is not enough of a way to live a life, and so I take Christianity as the way I try in my good moments to live. Hence insofar as the book describes Christianity, it is affirmative of my life and therefore autobiographical.

Autobiography cannot ever be separated form other people's stories and neither, ultimately, can the affirmative things in one's life. There's been much affirmative in my life, and I've had many teachers in the faith and in philosophy, not all of them intending to teach but who taught nonetheless. Here are a few. Susan McLeod-Harrison, my bride, soul-mate, and woman of courage. She means more to me than I could ever have imagined when we met over eight years ago. I cannot say enough of her good character. She has helped me be a better person, and has helped me be healed in many ways. Ian McLeod, my eldest, has ceased dancing in my living room by growing up to adulthood, leaving home, and getting married, but I cherish his friendship. Micah McLeod-Harrison, my youngest, who dances for Susan and me, and who truly makes me laugh.

Others include Steve Fratt, lover of all things military, save the horror. Elfrieda Harvie, my "second mom" during high school, long gone to God, who suffered inestimably, but whose faith inspired me. Charlie Kamilos,

---

1. Chesterton, *Orthodoxy*, 6.

spiritual director. John and Ginny Murray, whose house I remodeled, and therein was privileged to watch a family in love. Andy Oliver with whom I played as a child and who remains my friend. Fr. John Padgett, who once appeared as Christ to me. Rev. Curt Peterson, who asked me, when I was discouraged about the faith, who my theologians were, to which I had to reply that I'd been reading death of God theology. JoAnne Harrison, my mother-in-law, who read the book in manuscript and made helpful suggestions even though, as she said on reading it, the book is a "hickory nut above my persimmon." Somehow I doubt that. Jean McLeod, my mother, who changed my diapers, worried when I didn't come home on time, and with much grace helped me walk through my grief at my late wife's death. Norman McLeod, my father, who taught me how to move through what life throws you, and do it with laughter, and who now is laughing with Jesus. Rebecca McLeod, my late wife, who suffered long and who, along with my father, is laughing with Jesus.

Significant portions of chapter 4 can be found in a chapter entitled "History, Humans and God" from my book *Make/Believing the World(s): Toward a Christian Ontological Pluralism* (Montreal: McGill-Queens University Press, 2009). I thank McGill-Queen's for their kind permission to reprint some of that work.

There are, of course, others. Many others—teachers, fellow-ministers, pastors, colleagues, friends and family. I'm sorry I can't list all of you. Not all will agree with these musings but I hope they enjoy them nonetheless. I thank them mostly for being friends and for sharing their stories with me.

1

Story

I HATE PARTIES. WELL, "HATE" is a strong term, one my mother and father taught me not to use. Without, I'm afraid, as much success as they might have liked. So, trying to be a little more pleasant, let me say, instead, that for me, party-going with strangers is less than pleasant. It's not just that my introverted side comes out in such settings or that my sometime native longing for the interior life is most apparent under party-type scrutiny. The real issue is the inevitable question, "what do you do for a living?"

I'm stuck. I can't get out of it. I've got to say something. I always hope my next line won't bring out what I call "the dreaded conversation." So I squirm. I'd like to change the subject, but typically fail. I squirm some more and then finally settle on something about working at a university. Not good enough. My interlocutor wants more, and I start feeling a little like one of Socrates' philosophical conversational partners—uncomfortable because I know that more likely than not I'm about to be on the mean end of a gadfly's bite. "What do you do at the university?" So I own up—partly. I let out that I teach. "What?" comes the friendly but fated question. In a muted tone I've learned through too many parties, I usually manage to get out the doomed word "philosophy." I hope what my conversation partner hears is "psychology" or "physiology" or "philanthropy." I don't really care, so long as it's anything but "philosophy."

For all the noise at parties, however, my interlocutor's hearing is most often excellent. I brace myself for the following retorts: "Oh, I had a philosophy class once. I hated it." Or, "I had a philosophy class once. I didn't understand a thing." Or, "I had a philosophy class once. I was so glad when it was over. I never did get the point." Sometimes the term "philosophy" draws more positive responses, but in my experience the downbeats outweigh the upbeats.

Although touting itself as a love of wisdom, philosophy strikes many as removed, distant, and, sometimes, flat-out dull. A philosophy colleague of mine once said he'd rather read a novel than a philosophical essay. Another one said that contemporary philosophy often "runs from wisdom." I agree. Reading philosophy is not nearly as enjoyable as a good novel; and if it's not running from wisdom, it is often ducking the curves wisdom throws. Does anyone read philosophy for fun? For most people, talking philosophy is simply not as pleasant as watching a movie or attending a play. Where is the connection between philosophical ideas and the life we live? Where is the wisdom so earnestly sought by Plato, Augustine, or Hildegard? As someone who spends a great deal of time with the complexity of philosophical thought, I still long for words to communicate wisdom in helpful ways.

We live by story. Indeed, each human life is a story, filled with hoping, dreaming, suffering, truth-telling, laughing, fiction-making, fact-finding, living, and dying. Part of my story includes being trained to tell very complicated, abstract, philosophical tales. Unfortunately, only a few care to cozy up to fire where I find so much warmth. Somewhere in the complexity, the story line is easily lost, and wisdom oft-time runs to hide. When I began to teach, I felt I was floundering and that thereby my students were likely to flounder too. I wanted them not just to walk away with the distinctions and subtleties of logic, but with changed hearts. I longed to tell a different kind of story, one nearby, close to hearth and fire. I wanted to speak the wisdom I felt I occasionally had glimmers of, not because the wisdom was mine, but because somehow, my story was my students' story too. So my teaching increasingly became embroidered by stories.

When Socrates, the voice of Plato, was asked to tell the audience what the Good is, he said he couldn't give a *logos* (a philosophical account) but only a *mythos* (a story). Hence was born the Myth of the Cave wherein we hear of people saving themselves out of ignorance and into the light of the Good. One moral of Plato's story—not emphasized enough—is that when it comes to the Good—the really important stuff—only a story will do! Yet any philosophical happiness to be found in the story is found only, it seems, if the story is a lived one. The whole point of the Myth of the Cave is to encourage the listeners to engage in a life of philosophy, to search actively for wisdom. Yet not just any story will do. Or so I will suggest. Fiction, while teaching us, ultimately derives from history, from factuality, from our lives. It is our lives that are important. But unlike in the Myth of the Cave, where a lone thinker works her way to the light, the really important stories are told in common. They are history. For philosophy ultimately to help, its truth must be communicated by the common story we call history, and a particular kind of history at that. At its best, I believe philosophy must be deeply autobiographical, if it is really to communicate, really to help change the hearts of others.

What kind of autobiography? Of the rich, the famous, the powerful? Most of us certainly are none of those things. And in what way can philosophy be autobiographical? Often people say philosophy is irrelevant or not practical. But I wonder then about philosophical ideas such as God, democracy, and free will? What of their negations—atheism, totalitarianism, and coercion? What of the myriad of other alternatives? Aren't these ideas the most concrete and practical of all? What kind of influence do such ideas have in the world? Ultimately, aren't each of these sorts of ideas the basis for culture and ultimately for individual lives, and hence the basis of everyone's autobiography?

Dorothy Sayers noted that only a god should write autobiography. She was right. But fools rush in where angels fear to tread. A fool sometimes sees things the rest of us can't, or maybe the fool just says what needs to be said, consequences notwithstanding. Like Jeremiah the prophet, fools sometimes get themselves thrown into pits and left to rot. Yet prophets we need, and suffering fools isn't always bad for, like children, sometimes they say the most profound things. So I ask you to suffer with me for a while, waiting to see if perhaps, in my foolish muttering, something of value might emerge.

Autobiography is, of course, history, and history is a kind of memory rooted in life lived. Yet autobiography is inseparable from the truth of the others in one's life. Socrates never wrote anything, and Jesus wrote only a few words in the sand. How can two of the most influential people in Western culture have shaped us so much, with nary a note written? The answer is brief and yet complicated: their lives spoke truth and reality into the lives of others. The intellectual autobiography of Plato tells us of Socrates, and the biographies of the early Christians tell us of Jesus. Indeed, one's autobiography is mostly biography, a kind of common memory.

Autobiography is hence not separable from history and larger cultural questions. At one point, in the context of writing about memory, St. Augustine said of God, "while you were within me, I was outside."[1] The difficulty of these words, the complexity of these words, overwhelms. At this point in Augustine's text, he has admitted that God was in his memory only after Augustine met "the divine Beauty" and yet Augustine remains puzzled how God could be in Augustine at all. How can God be inside me, while I am not? The matter is no less complicated if we replace the "me" with how can God be in my memory when I am not or even further, how can God be in (my) history when I am not? By rewriting Augustine's question, we raise what I think is a central question for us at this point in history and we move his question from the personal to the public. Understood in that way, I think Augustine's question is as profound today as it was when he penned it.

We speak of the postmodern world in which we live, but few can agree over what that world is. To be postmodern we must obviously have once been modern. Painting in very broad strokes, modernism can be characterized as the world of pure reason, with a deep commitment to a peculiar understanding of scientific methodology, an understanding verging on scientism rather than science, and a nearly religious belief in objectivity. What is true (the way the world is) and truths themselves (our descriptions of the world) generally do not depend upon human perspectives. In contrast, the radical postmodern (and I do mean radical, for I have myself proposed a moderate sort of postmodernism, hints of which are found in the following pages)[2] is taken with a sort of anti-reason, a deep undercurrent of subjectivity, and a profound fictional-

---

1. Augustine *Confessions* 10.27.38 (Ryan, 254).

2. See McLeod-Harrison, *Make/believing the World(s)*. Often the road less taken is just the middle road. In most ways, the postmodernism I propose in some of my other publications is a moderate one. But those publications are quite technical and written for the professional philosopher. Here I try to make that moderate road more intuitive and more understandable to the average, non-technically trained reader. That, at least, is my goal.

ization of the world. In radical postmodernism, everything depends on human perspectives.

In experience, I think we live in neither of these worlds, but in both. We strive to understand history—our histories—in the midst of the struggle between the modern and radical postmodern sirens calling out to us. We struggle, indeed, to understand ourselves and how we are to live. What does it mean to be a human who stands between simply receiving the cold, hard deliverances of reason and scientism, on the one hand, and making things up out of whole cloth on the other? What does it mean to be a human who stands between the cold objectivity of the modern and the radical fictionalization of the postmodern?

We have lost our history, and while all things ultimately meaningful are in history, we are outside, either in some fiction or in some objectified version of the empirical, physicality of the world. This is a book about getting back inside history, where meaningfulness, happiness, and ultimately God are to be found. This book is an answer to my party-going peers when they ask me "what do you do for a living?" Partly cultural critique, partly philosophy, partly theological, and, I hope, deeply Christian, these pages are filled with story. The story is mostly an apology for my faith as a Christian philosopher. What sort of apology? Most directly, it is an apology in Socrates' sense of the word, a defense or account of a life lived philosophically. But it is a defense not just of a philosophical life but of a Christian philosophical life. But ultimately it is not a defense of my little life but of the life of God and, in particular, the Christian God. Yet I don't argue for God's existence, or for the historicity of the resurrection of Jesus, or for any of the traditional things Christian apologists usually try to show. The book is more a collection of explanatory road maps. Maps are historically rooted, and they bespeak stories and contexts. Nevertheless, I hope the legend is clear enough and that it points in the right directions. While I've endeavored to say some things that point toward wisdom, I hope at least to have said some things that are true.

What I write is a more publically accessible attempt to do what I have elsewhere called "pastoral philosophy."[3] The reader should be under no illusion that what follows is a romp through events in my life, that is, traditional autobiography of a typical sort. Rather it is some ideas in which I share bits and pieces of my life but also bits and pieces

---

3. See McLeod-Harrison, *Repairing Eden*.

of philosophy aimed at the public with a view toward encouraging others to live a truly philosophical life, a life of wisdom found in living with God in history. I want the essay to be one voice in the postmodern discussion and I deeply hope it is a voice of wisdom learned through living life grounded in the wisdom of history.

Now on to the tale.

2

Fiction

I'M JEALOUS. IT WOULDN'T be so bad if the source of my jealousy weren't so close to home. My wife, you see, writes a terrific short story, and I'm jealous. Although I've written and even published some poetry, I would have liked to be a fiction writer. Of course, it's not the money. One of my colleagues—a first-rate poet/song writer—has noted about writing poetry that "one can make dozens of dollars."[1] One would expect not much more to be made out of fiction writing and I know from experience that not only does philosophy bake no bread, but it doesn't typically make even dozens of dollars. (I've often thought of retiring early and opening up a bakery called "Who Says Philosophy Bakes No Bread?" but I've not yet convinced myself that baking will generate more than dozens of dollars either!)

Back to fiction writing. I don't have it in me. My attempts at fiction are duller than a three-year old razor. But I love to read fiction—sometimes a little too much. It's not uncommon for me to ignore the philosophy I need to read in order to finish the novel of the week (or of the weekend!). In fact, it's a wonder I've read or written any philosophy at all. But reading fiction and writing it, no matter what the fiction-writing manuals hint at, just don't seem related to me. One I can do with ease, the other not at all. Yet sometimes philosophy is like fiction. I think, in fact, that the most radical kinds of postmodern philosophy push us toward the fictional, at least metaphorically. I believe, in short, that fiction

---

1. To be attributed to poet, scholar, and singer of songs that love peace, William Joliff.

is a good symbol for the most radical postmodernisms we find. So in good philosophical fashion, although I can't and don't write fiction, I can sure philosophize about it! Let's see what we can learn about ourselves by thinking about fiction.

Consider Elaine Risley who expresses her frustration when she utters ". . . post this, post that. Everything is post these days, as if we're all just a footnote to something earlier that was real enough to have a name of its own." Risley's insight strikes the ear as powerful in its discrimination, as well as its expansiveness. A few words, an emphasis or two, and not only our world but *we* are exposed. Like a film's negative, the exposure transposes our order of seeing. The exposure highlights, by an availing reversal, both our nakedness and our dressiness. Our world, long since fading, and we who sing in its chorus, are dressed for the drama only to discover it cancelled, and perhaps ourselves with it. The Emperor's postmodern clothes gussy us up. At least the traditional Emperor had his nakedness with which to cover his shame. When *we* shed our clothes, we find not even our nakedness. We find nothing at all, not even our shame.

The power of Risley's analysis lies not only in her observation of the derivative nature of the prefix "post," and not only in her suggestion that if a thing is real enough, it can bear a name of its own. The power expands from the very nature of Elaine Risley herself. For Elaine Risley is a fictional being, the main character in the novel, *Cat's Eye,* a creation of Margaret Atwood.[2]

But Risley, for all her fictionality, is not unreal. Some strange kind of being attends her, some kind of reality with which we novel readers are familiar. Risley is Canadian, not American or French or Nigerian. Risley is female, although her brother is not. Not unimportantly, he is killed in a senseless plane hijacking, his body falling to the tarmac below the plane's open passenger door.[3] This is, Risley says, how her brother enters the past. Risley grew up breathing deep the fulsome odors of the laboratories at the University of Toronto, and cavorting through fields gathering bugs with her scientist father. She swam in icy Lake Superior, lived in old mining camps, and rode in the back seat of her parent's car

---

2. The opening quotation is from Atwood, *Cat's Eye,* 90.

3. Risley, the fictional character, fictionalizes her brother's end, at least some of it. What status does this fiction within a fiction have? See also the insightful comments of Eco, *Six Walks in the Fictional Woods.*

while her brother and friends spoke pig Latin one to another. Had Risley lacked any of these things, she wouldn't be Risley. Nor would any other fictional being be what it is, were it to lack the central properties it has. Huck Finn could not be a slave, nor could Jane Eyre be from Brazil.[4] Should any of us think otherwise, try passing a literature examination on *Huck Finn* in which one's thesis is that Huck is really a black slave just as his friend Jim.

Yet we are suspicious here. Surely fictional creatures can be other than what they are. After all, we make them up. The ambiguity of the following statement exposes the paradox: Fictional beings can't be anything. On the one hand, fictional beings can't *be* anything, for they are not real. On the other hand, fictional beings can't be *anything*, for they are cemented by the frame of their texts or stories. And yet that fictional beings can't *be* seems to imply that they can, in fact, be *anything*. Surely, one might say, the fictional being's creator can make the character do or say *anything*.

There's the rub. Not even the creator of a character totally controls the character. Necessity is necessary, even in novels and fairy tales. Mathematical notions, and truly logical notions, are one and the same, *necessary*. If all As are Bs, and there are some As, then those As are Bs.[5] Of course, the fiction writer can say things like, "well, Jill lived in a world in which all As are Bs, but even though this is an A, it is not a B," but to what does this come? I can dream *that* I squared the circle, but I cannot dream *squaring* the circle. Certain clear limits upon what can happen emerge, even within the walls of a fictional house.

I won't debate here the laws of logic or their inexorability. The most radical of postmodern philosophers use logic, even while denying its usefulness. But another corner of the fictional house remains unswept. Must the laws of nature be followed? Does the apple *have to*

---

4. In these last two sentences, I've freely gone between "would have" and "could have," difficult terms both. See some interesting comments on these terms in Austin, "Ifs and Cans."

5. "There are certain sequences or developments . . . which are, in the true sense of the word, reasonable. They are, in the true sense of the word, necessary. Such are mathematical and merely logical sequences. We in fairyland (who are the most reasonable of all creatures) admit that reason and that necessity. For instance, if the Ugly Sisters are older than Cinderella, it is (in an iron clad and awful sense) *necessary* that Cinderella is younger than the Ugly Sisters . . . . If Jack is the son of a miller, then a miller is the father of Jack." Chesterton, *Orthodoxy*, 50.

fall off the tree? Well, no, it doesn't. No true necessity exists here. As any good scientist knows, all kinds of weird things can (and do!) happen in nature. Predictability isn't as neat as we'd like.[6] Why can't nature produce apples on the tusks of elephants every once in a while? I like the thought of God bent over in the garden making the daisies new and fresh every morning, one at a time.[7]

Yet this isn't quite right either. Huck Finn and Elaine Risley can't be anything at all. Huck must be from the South and Elaine must be from Canada. What does "must" mean in that last sentence? It isn't the "must" of reason and necessity, some following of the laws of logic, for there is a clear sense in which Huck need not be from the South, anymore than cows have to moo rather than bark.[8] Novel readers know better.[9] Nor is the "must" one of physical necessity, as our scientific and naturalistic friends would have it. G. K. Chesterton writes:

> Here is the peculiar perfection of tone and truth in the nursery tales. The man of science says, "Cut the stalk, and the apple will fall"; but he says it calmly, as if the one idea really led up to the other. The witch in the fairy tale says, "Blow the horn, and the ogre's castle will fall"; but she does not say it as if it were something in which the effect obviously arose out of the cause. Doubtless she has given the advice to many champions, and has seen many castles fall, but she does not lose either her wonder or her reason. She does not muddle her head until it imagines a necessary mental connection between a horn and a falling tower.

---

6. Again, Chesterton, *Orthodoxy*, 50, 51: "But as I put my head over the hedge of the elves and began to take notice of the natural world, I observed an extraordinary thing. I observed that learned men in spectacles were talking of the actual things that happened—dawn and death and so on—as if *they* were rational and inevitable. They talked as if the fact that trees bear fruit were just as *necessary* as the fact that two and one trees make three. But it is not. There is an enormous difference by the test of fairyland; which is the test of the imagination. You cannot *imagine* two and one not making three. But you can easily imagine trees not growing fruit; you can imagine them growing golden candlesticks or tigers hanging on by the tail. . . . We have always in our fairy tales kept this sharp distinction between the science of mental relations, in which there really are laws, and the science of physical facts, in which there are no laws, but only weird repetitions."

7. See Chesterton, *Orthodoxy*, 60.

8. It is of note that the sounds we take animals to make vary culturally. The Japanese represent the sound animals make quite differently than do English speakers.

9. Indeed, a novel must surprise if it is to stand on its own two feet as a novel. One suspects a connection between the terms "novel" (as in fiction) and "novel" (as in new).

But the scientific men do muddle their heads, until they imagine a necessary mental connection between an apple leaving the tree and an apple reaching the ground.[10]

One cannot analyze "Huck Finn" and get "born and raised in the South," anymore than one can get "must fall to the ground" out of "apple." And one's tone of voice doesn't change that fact. Yet Huck Finn *must* be from the South and Elaine Risley from Canada. They and their natures are "fixed" in some way. Could this "fixedness" be the "must" of historical fact, the "giveness" of the empirical data?[11] Once the apple fell, it fell. No wishful thinking will change *that* fact; no interpretation will undo *that* data. Yet while historical "musts" clearly cannot be changed in real life, they apparently can in novels, or at least in fairy tales. The princess loved the prince and he loved her and one time can be replaced by another time, and all the horrible things that happened to make the prince a toad never happened. This is more than just the prince and princess starting anew. Indeed, the prince and the princess *never lived through this time before*. Neither the prince nor the princess remembers the horror, for it never happened. Historians, unlike fiction writers, cannot wave their wands and produce *that* kind of magic.

One difference between history and fiction is that the fiction writer *makes up* her empirical facts. She has no "given" data with which to work. The fiction writer knows no necessary connection between apples and falling downward and so can set the frame and pattern of the story any way she desires, save for the hurdles of logic. The historian, who also knows no necessary connection between apples and falling down, remains bound by what happened—what we call "the empirical data." The apple did indeed fall. The historian must therefore report and not create the empirical facts. She must not make up her data out of whole cloth, even if she makes her story up from reweaving, patching, and stitching together *pieces* of cloth.[12] Therefore the frame and pattern of

---

10. Chesterton, *Orthodoxy*, 51.

11. Here let me beg some difficult philosophical questions, such as what makes a historical fact a fact, or what counts as data. Let me suggest, minimally, that the historian must face the court of the empirical at some point, and wherever that point is, it is unmovable. Either the event occurred or it did not, either the historical documents record it, or they do not, the historian's evidential and interpretive difficulties notwithstanding. More on this below.

12. The historian does much more than report. Mere reports of the data do not a history make. Reports are chronologies, not histories. Again, more on this below.

the story is more determinate, more exterior, for the historian than for the fiction writer. Jimmy Carter grew up in the South. So did Huck Finn. And that makes all the difference in regard to who Carter and Huck are, so far as the historian or fiction writer respectively is concerned. But the historian isn't free to change her data in telling Carter's story, whereas Samuel Clemens could freely change his facts. Reality fixes the "must" of (contingent) historical fact in a way that reality does not fix the "must" of fiction. Yet the facts of fiction are no more malleable than the facts of history. If Atwood began with Risley as a Nigerian, then other things would follow. Or if Clemens began Huck's life as a Native American we would read a very different *Huck Finn*—indeed, not *Huck Finn* at all.

The characters in novels or fairy tales do not follow their own devices. While we intuitively expect fictional creatures to be entirely free, they are not. Fictional creatures cannot do whatever they want. They are, once their empirical facts are set, stuck. They follow their own fictional "must." The novelist can make up the tale and its characters any way she wants; but once the fictional being's nature and world is formed, its nature and world are fixed, more or less the way historical facts are fixed.

I say "more or less" for they are not the same. The novel, once written (and published?), is fixed in a way history is not. The fictional "must" is a "must" set by contingencies *outside* the novel—that is, fictional "musts" are set by the author, not the characters—and the tale comes to an end.[13] Elaine Risley's being is *permanently* fixed. She must be Canadian, just as Jimmy Carter must be from the South. Yet Risley is what she is not just in this detail but in *all* details. Risley has no future to determine herself. She simply has no *future* to determine, for she isn't temporal as are we. To determine is to choose, and to choose implies a future with all its goals and activities. Risley has no future. She can't determine or choose anything. She therefore cannot *determine* herself. One's future, insofar as it is one's *personal* future, seems to depend on one's ability to choose. If one can't choose for oneself, one becomes a slave to contingencies out of one's control and one has no future *of one's own*. Risley cannot choose or determine anything about herself—she literally has no future. So, Risley has no future to determine herself. She lives with facts fixed from the

---

13. Fiction writers sometimes speak as if their characters "write" the story, sounding, thereby, as if the characters have freewill. But surely not, except perhaps in a way discussed by Dorothy Sayers, *Mind of the Maker*, 61–84. The freewill of the character, Sayers says, is an extension of the author's personality.

outside. Historical facts, in contrast, are not all fixed from the outside. Some are, such as that Jimmy Carter was born in the South. Carter had no choice where he was born, or who his parents were, or how tall his genetic code would make him. But Carter sometimes chooses the details. He can decide where to live, or whether to obey his parents, or to purchase clothes that fit his genetically determined stature. History opens to the future.[14] Real humans are not stuck. We are free, if not entirely, then at least in important ways that Risley, Huck, and their myriads of cohorts are not. Risley or Huck cannot be anything other than the limits of their fictional worlds allow. Margaret Atwood, Samuel Clemens, and their muses pulled all the strings and then cut them the minute the book was sent in final proof form back to the publisher. Risley ends where the last page of Atwood's book ends, unless Atwood writes another novel where Risley reappears, as if rejuvenated from some sort of cryogenic suspension. Huck not only hails from the South, but he must stay in the South. Real humans are not so tied down. Our parents made us, to be sure. But no strings are being pulled (although some are attached). Our borders are more flexible, more creative than those of fictional beings. The future runs in continuity with history for real humans, in a way that it doesn't for fictional humans. The "musts" of fiction and the "musts" of historical facts and data are not the same.

Risley wonderfully characterizes the fictional space of the "posts." But her characterization is particularly well adapted to radical postmodernism. Risley expresses this by the exasperated tone in her voice: ". . . post this, post that." This exasperation is born of sheer exhaustion. Like Elaine Risley, we are tired. We ran the modern race. While some ran against its rejection of the supernatural, its naturalistic readings of the world, or its "liberal" approach to human freedoms, others ran for its justice, its universal rationality, or its goals of peace and freedom. Just as we caught up, we found the race track switched. No longer modern, the track is postmodern. Radical postmodern tracks aren't clearly marked, they lack guard rails or borders; indeed, they lack stable footing altogether.

Risley expresses the derivative nature of the name "postmodern." Not just some technical pronouncement, hers is a sigh, an almost gasping lament. "Post this, post that. Everything is post these days, as if we're

---

14. There is more to say here too, but as I've already indicated in the notes, history deserves its own chapter. Suffice it to say that history is both being made and being written, but the two are not the same.

all just a footnote to something earlier that was real enough to have a name of its own." Notice the shift from "this" and "that" and "thing" to "we"; a subtle shift, easily missed. It is, however, quintessentially and radically postmodern.[15] *Things* have lost their substantiality. Only *we* are left. Risley's only mistake may be, in fact, the "we."[16] Perhaps the radical postmodern just leaves an "I." It's as if *I* am not real enough to have a name of my own.

The quintessential modern viewed the world and himself through the eyes of Rene Descartes. "I think, therefore I am" rallies the world around *my* existence. From myself, I move to God as other, and at last to the outer, external world as other. But for the radical postmodern, these things are fictional at best, determined by me. And then even *I* may not be. Even solipsism[17] loses its lonely grasp. What is the "I," if not a construction of the social, the public? But since the whole is unreal, what can I be? At best, God, the world, and even I are nothing but a name.

Risley rightly connects the name of a thing to its reality. What we've lost isn't just our reality. We've lost the capacity to bear a name of our own. But if Risley accurately perceives the radical postmodern situation, she also rightly notices that it's *as if* the past had a reality. A radical postmodern understanding of the "world," one supposes, can't allow things from the past to be any more real than we are. Risley wonderfully nuances the postmodern situation as reflection—a doubly exposed negative. When read carefully, Risley's claim doesn't affirm the past in some wistful way. No, the postmodern can't do that. No past exists to wist. Even the "post" nature of the postmodern is a construction of a wisting. The radical postmodern wishes for reality, longs for a past, but has neither.

Radical postmodernism leaves many of us uncomfortable, feeling vague, unsure of ourselves and our world. Whence this vagueness? What do we fear in radical postmodernism? Nothing, nothing at all. That is the "basis" for the fear: that there is nothing, nothing beside me and my beliefs, me and my theories, me and my words—and perhaps not even a me. I have a name, but I don't have a self. No link connects the name of a thing and reality. Only the name echoes. So, radical postmodernism

---

15. It's odd to use any relative of "essential" when speaking of the postmodern. The irony is, I hope, not lost.

16. What is the status of a fictional "mistake?"

17. Solipsism is the view that only I and my ideas exist.

is a heresy (even though its less radical cousins are not). Radical postmodernism places us mortals above the Real. Radical postmodernism's heretical suggestions spring from its emphasis on the name alone. Yet this is too simple. We long to occupy the space of the Real, the Solid, the Impassable. But that, too, is too simple. Truth lies in the mean, in the peculiar space *between* the real objective world of things—the modern—and the fictional world of names—the radical postmodern. The space has a name. It's called history. But first, something more on naming.

3

Naming

My mother waited until I was in my thirties to tell the story of my name. I've wondered what significance there is to that fact, but I won't speculate here. Let's just hear the story of my name. When I was born my parents named me Mark Stephen McLeod. Or so I thought until my mother's confession. My father's name was "Norman." (He had no middle name—is there a story there?) Apparently when the hospital staff asked what name to put on the form for the birth certificate, they heard "Mark Stephen McLeod" whereas my parents said "Mark Norman McLeod." Now that, in itself, isn't so strange or startling. What is a bit shocking is that once my parents received the official birth certificate from the Province of Ontario, they didn't bother to correct it! So instead of being named after my father (of which I would have been proud) I'm named after a biblical character. I've often teased my mother that she apparently didn't love me enough to give me my proper name, or that she thought more highly of the biblical Stephen than her own husband and my father.

Now lest you think this humorous story is also trivial or that names are not important (a rose by any other name is still a rose), consider this. As I grew up, I always thought my parents had given a great deal of consideration to my name. Hence I thought it valuable to think of myself not only as Mark (as in St. Mark—a sort of "junior" to St. Peter's "senior") but as Stephen, the first recorded martyr of the Christian faith. Stephen was a person of great faith and courage and, in at least some minor (if largely unsuccessful) ways, I've tried to think of myself as attempting to live up to his name. How differently would I have thought of myself with my father's name rather than Stephen's? Not that my father wasn't a saint—but that is best left up to God.

My name is now Mark Stephen McLeod-Harrison. My wife Susan and I "met" each other via the web. I posted myself as someone, among other things, who was interested in a relationship with a Christian woman who was a feminist. Well, she meets that expectation. Not too long after we were engaged, she and I were out for a walk. She asked me, rather nonchalantly, if we would hyphenate our names. I said sure. Then she wanted to know if her name could go last, since typically the woman's name goes first and often gets lost. Being a feminist myself, I said "sure." So I am now known by my new name "Mark McLeod-Harrison" and students regularly drop the "McLeod" out. And my mother, bless her heart but she's not alone, continues to call me "McLeod" rather than "McLeod-Harrison." People just don't seem to want to adjust to the idea that I have a different, improved name.

But what is, after all, in a name—or in naming? Genesis 2 has it that God created the heavens and the earth but neither shrub nor plant sprung up. Nothing grew because God had sent no rain and no human worked the ground. One wonders why a human needed to work the ground, for we know full well that plants need earth and water to grow, but humans are not a necessary part of the picture. But the situation was more complicated than that. We are told that although water was not present in the form of rain, it was present because of streams coming up from the ground. These streams watered the whole surface of the earth. So water was present, even if not in the form of rain, and earth was present. Why did the plants not sprout? We are left with this: no human worked the ground.

What is the importance of the human? While surely no human is necessary for plants to grow, humans are necessary for gardens to grow. It was a garden God wanted. Gardens have order and order requires meaning. For meaning, one needs people.

The story continues with the creation of *adam* (the man, the common noun "man," that is, "the man," not the proper name, Adam nor Man). God formed *adam* from the dust of the ground and breathed life into *adam*'s nostrils, and *adam* became a living soul. God placed *adam* into a garden God made in the East, in Eden. God then made the trees grow out of the ground, trees of all kinds, trees pleasing to the eye and good for food. So, God made *adam* and placed *adam* into the Garden. *adam* watched as God made the trees grow out of the ground. God spoke and there were trees. The image comes to mind of God and *adam* walking around the Garden together, God saying "how about the pomegranate tree here and the fig tree there?" *adam* replies "yes, that would be a fine place for the figs, but why not put the figs closer to the grapes?" The show began, God uttering earthly being into place: "Trees: pomegranate here, fig there," shouted God, like a waiter in a short-order restaurant. Erupting up through the soil blasted two trees, a pomegranate and a fig, growing faster than any plant on time-elapsed film. God continued the divine work with spruce and pine, orange and pepper, hazelnut and plum. As this fireworks of fruit came nearly to an end, and the Garden's perimeters were filled, God and *adam* strolled to the middle of the Garden. Without asking *adam*, God gently, sadly, whispered, "trees: knowledge of good and evil, life." Up sprang *adam*'s future, full bloom and beautiful.

A river flowed from Eden to water the Garden. God placed *adam* in the Garden to work and tend it. While set there to work, God gave *adam* all the fruit of the trees to eat save for one. Snacking on the fruit from the tree of the knowledge of good and evil was proscribed. Of this tree, *adam* was told, when you eat of it you will surely die.

One imagines *adam* setting out to work, wielding his tools, trimming branches here, splicing new fruit there, and tilling the ground all around. But other work awaited him. God saw *adam* alone and noted this lack of goodness. So God set out on some work of God's own, making *adam* a suitable helper. Once again, God and *adam* were together, and God created things. The making, however, was not a speaking on God's part. Instead, God scraped together dust and dirt to form the beasts of the fields and the birds of the air. As God shaped the animals, something new was afoot, and it was not just the animals. The world was about to see a wondrous thing. While the creation of the animals themselves amazes, what God did with them was more profound. God brought the animals to *adam* to see what *adam* would name them, and the world was never the same again. God let *adam* speak the animals into completion.

Picture this. God waiting expectantly for each name like a young child awaiting a gift she's been told she's about to receive. More curious is the fact that *adam* was not instructed to name. *adam* apparently knew to do this, it was natural to *adam*. *adam* knew it was within *adam's* power, that it was a good thing. So God brought the animals to *adam* to hear the name. *adam* worked a new garden. *adam's* work was the wielding of words: *adam* trimmed, spliced, and tilled the words, blessing the world with name and symbol, with lion and tiger, with elephant, alligator, and basset hound. Whatever *adam* called an animal, that became its name. God gave *adam* a role in creation; *adam* named the animals. *adam* named the livestock, the birds of the air, and the beasts of the field. It is of note that between God's creating animals and birds and *adam's* naming them, a third category is added: livestock. Where did livestock come from, if not from naming? Humans have the power to name and thereby create. What is this naming? Whence its power, its magic, its mystery?

Walker Percy tells us naming cannot be understood as another scientific, causal function, like explaining why stars go nova. Not an interaction, naming is an affirmation. Percy tells us naming may be defined as the affirmation of the thing as being what it is under the auspices of the name. The suggestion that naming is an affirmation is pregnant with truth. Percy tells us that with naming comes a new orientation, an orientation not merely biological but ontological; it is not science at issue, but being at stake; it is not words about life (*bios*) but words about being (*ontos*). Words are ontological (words about being: a definition and a truth). To name, then, is to affirm being. Percy says the act of affirmation is a yes-saying, and yes-sayings require two people, one to affirm and the other to hear. "Yes" can only be said *by* a person *to* a person. The ontological orientation rests in the need to affirm, for both of us, what a thing is. In symbolizing a thing we lay alongside that thing a name, a symbol. This laying alongside occurs via the copula, the simple "is." The "frog" in the sentence, "that is a frog" is not a frog; it is a word, a name. The *is* is not the *is* of real identity (as we are taught in logic, that A = A) but of the intentional relation of identity. Perhaps we should name it "the *is* of naming." When our corporate human need to affirm things comes into play as we learn to name things (and *vice versa*), we become different kinds of beings ourselves. No longer just biological entities, we become entities capable of authenticity and inauthenticity. We are no longer merely biological but normative. We live authentically in the joy of naming. We live inauthentically when being is lost under the symbol.

"It's only a sparrow" indicates the loss of being. We can, Percy says, dispose of things under their symbols.[1]

Back to the Garden, the work of words, and the naming of the animals. In all this naming frenzy, no suitable helper for *adam* is found. So God makes another creature, coming not from the humus but the human—*adam's* side, *adam's* rib. *adam* calls her *ishshah* for she is taken out of *ish*. The woman is not like the other animals, she is like *ish*. "Woman" and "man" are related terms in English, and so they are in Hebrew. It is not until Genesis 2:23 that the term *ish* appears. Until then the man is referred to as *adam*. So *ish* and *ishshah* are not proper names. They simply note the sameness of the man and the woman. She is not made of the ground as animals are made. She is made bone of bone, flesh of flesh, *ishshah* of *ish*, woman of man. It is still generic, just as *adam* is until later in the text. Indeed, *adam* doesn't name the woman the woman, for the term *ishshah* is used before *adam* uses it, for it appears in verse 22.

As Gilbert Bilezikian[2] points out, if the use of *ishshah* is a naming, it is not like the naming of the animals. When *adam* names the animals, their kind of being is created, or at least shaped, by the naming. The naming of the woman is unlike the naming of the animals in that *adam* understands the woman to be like him and so uses a term that sounds like what he calls himself. This is vital: *ish* as a name doesn't show up until *ishshah* shows up. But *ishshah* is mentioned in the text before *ish*. In using the term *ishshah* (woman) first, *adam* names himself *ish* after her. She shares her name with him, recognizing her relatedness to him and yet also her difference from him. *adam* does not here give the woman a personal, individual name, any more than he gives personal, individual names to the animals. He names what is presented to him by the Creator; he names *kinds* of things and in so doing, names himself.

Yet, *adam* does name the woman with a proper name. Later, in the context of the Fall and the Curse, *adam* names the woman "Eve" (*hawwa*, which sounds like *hayya*, the term for "living") for it is from Eve that the living will come. It is, perhaps, a name of honor, for death has entered the world and "Eve" echoes the only way to new life. Yet no mention is made of God presenting Eve to *adam* for a name, no hint of God waiting with bated breath to see how creative *adam* can be. After the Fall, *adam*

---

1. Percy, "Naming and Being."
2. Bilezikian, *Beyond Sex Roles*. Several of the arguments about the use of Hebrew words in Genesis are his.

just names the woman "Eve." One reading of the text is that *adam* usurps the power, the mystery, the magic of creation. Just as God speaks the world into existence, so Adam "speaks" Eve into existence. Name-giving it is, but is it good? God gives *adam* some creative power. *adam* uses it, post-Fall, to name things without permission. Is this a type of control, an expression of *adam*'s desire to be like God, knowing good and evil? *adam* does not truly have the power to create Eve—but Adam assumes the power.

Who names *adam* Adam? *adam* just means "the man." It isn't until Gen 3:17 (when God pronounces on Adam the results of the Fall) that the article is dropped from *adam* and *adam* becomes Adam (like "the guy" becomes "Guy"[3]). "The man" simply becomes "Adam." *adam* has no name of his own. *adam* is a generic man. Adam, in fact, never receives a name of his own, not from the animals, not from the Serpent, not from Eve, and not from God. God uses the generic, dropping the article, and refers to *adam* as Adam. But is it a naming proper, a new creation? Or is it simply God's recognition of the new separation amongst the humans? The unnamed man—*adam*—suckles at the fruit. The generic man sets himself up to name good, to name evil, to name the world. While no sin exists in naming, as evidenced by God bringing the animals to Adam for names before the Fall, there is sin in certain kinds of naming. Naming abused is sin. Names have power. *adam*, when taking the fruit, puts himself above even God. After that, Adam names Eve. Such naming can be a kind of control, evidenced in names we call people we do not like, people we do not care about, or people we find ourselves fearing.

Another note from Percy. He says anxiety can occur when a person realizes that she or he cannot be named. The idea meshes well with the notion that the use of *ishshah* and *ish* is not a true naming. Neither can other namers be named. We are of a kind that cannot be named, that are not to be named as individuals. We are human, made in the image of God, female and male, permanently social. In the Garden, the woman, like the man, has a name in common with others—a name recognized by *adam* in the presence of God. Her first name is generic, universal, unified. The name is one of permanent community, charitable relationship. The name is not one of individuality. When Adam names the woman "Eve," does Adam step over his creative boundary? *Ishshah* is no longer simply woman, but Eve, a name given out of turn, the beginning of the

---

3. Ibid.

long Fall, the first step toward annihilation, the first step toward being alone, again. In the curse, God says the woman's desire will be for her husband and he will rule over her—a description (not a prescription) entailing tremendous ramifications. So, the naming of the woman as Eve is a mixed blessing. The name is an honor, recognizing her special role amongst the living. The naming makes her special, an individual. But she is controlled by this name, separated from the man, ruled over by the man. Adam becomes the naming manipulator. A new aloneness is created by this naming. Perhaps in naming the woman Eve, the man names himself Adam, isolating himself from Eve as he isolates *ish* from *ishshah*.

The challenge of naming manifests itself throughout human cultural development. The most recent manifestation of naming aloneness, and perhaps the most extreme, is the radical postmodern—words unchastened. Radical postmodernism is naming run amuck. Thus Percy's account is incomplete as it stands. In addition to an authentic and an inauthentic naming, there is also an annulling, a negating, a canceling naming. It begins with the naming of things unkindly, with malice, and extends to naming with manipulation and control. This is sin, perhaps at its most basic. In inauthentic naming, we lose being under the symbols. In annulment naming we dispose of being altogether with the symbols— by naming at first through destructive names: fatty, worthless, stupid, nigger, spic, chick, bitch, animal, wolf, prick. By these names we at first lose being, but later we annihilate being altogether as we come to think of names as reality itself. Radical postmodern naming, at its worst, is one step further from community. All words become words of power and control, words alone, without reality. The choice becomes not just a choice between authentic and inauthentic but amongst authentic, inauthentic, and annihilation. The radical postmodern at its worse pushes us into this last category, annihilation. While the use of pejorative names to control surfaced long ago, the radical postmodern moves us beyond the merely pejorative into the manipulative, for in the radical postmodern, a profound loss of the connection between true being and naming is recognized. We lose all possibility of integrity. When naming fails to affirm the being of what is, and names only the unreal, not only is the world lost, but we, too, are lost. Not only is community destroyed, but individuality as well. Integrity disintegrates for lack of the person.

Thus, radical postmodernism is a heresy not simply against religion but against our very being. No link remains between the name of a thing and reality. No link obtains not simply because we can't see the link, but because there is nothing real with which the link can relate. There is only the name. In radical postmodernism we mortals put ourselves above the Real, above the Other, much like *adam* puts himself above God in the story of the Garden. But *adam* was not postmodern. And Adam still recognized the Real, the Made, the Created-by-the-Other, even after the Fall. Adam simply wanted to control the Real his way and not God's. So Adam was not heretical. Radical postmodernism is heretical because it recognizes only the name, the power, the control of words and nothing else. The radical postmodern believes in nothing but the word and the creative power thereof. Words become the real; Reality is annihilated. Naming no longer affirms but annihilates. For the radical postmodern, the name, the word, is writ large and becomes the world. In the creation story, God's word has this power. *adam's* does not, although *adam's* word affects and changes the world. In radical postmodernism, the Word is demoted to the words. God disappears and the lonely human word replaces the divine.

4

History

THE IRONY OF MY writing a chapter *about* history (what history *is* rather than history itself) is that my early history with history is quite limited and, how shall I say it, quite dull. Perhaps not as dull as my fiction writing, but dull nevertheless.

My grade eleven history of Britain teacher read to us out of the textbook for a whole hour every day for a whole term. At least that's how I remember it, but history might belie my memory. When I changed high schools and found out I could drop history, it was the first to go— right after, I'm chagrined to say, French. My Bible college church history teacher did not have an advanced history degree and doubled as the college registrar. I got an A in the first term but a C in the second, not, I think, because of poorer performance but rather due to the fact that I registered for twenty-five hours or so of class that term so I could graduate early. When the teacher/registrar found out, he said that to do that much work in one term was not possible, even if practically permissible by the rules of "registraring." We argued but I ended up with the upper hand. Or so I thought. I signed up for the classes and did well in them all—except for, oddly enough, the second half of church history.

When I finally moved on to the liberal arts for my philosophy degree, I short-changed my history education by taking Western Civilization via the infamous "CLEP" exam. I just paid my twenty-five dollars, read through a textbook entitled something like "The Acme Shorter History of Western Civilization," took the multiple choice test, and passed. No sitting through what I thought would be three boring hours per week of dusty remembrances. In short, my history with history isn't good. Yet a number of my good friends have been historians, and of them I stand in awe. Just how do they know so much? On the loom of history, how do they create such colorful and oft-times beautiful patterns?

History is not a set of empirical facts. History is not the events of the past. History is not the data.[1] History is the story, the recounting, the telling of the past. What past? The human past. Prehistory ended when humans came to be. History began when humans began to speak it and eventually to write it. History is, nevertheless, constrained by empirical facts and data; it is obliged by them, beholden to them. History is bordered or hemmed in by the events of the past. History, to be history and not fiction, must have its past. But history must also create a story, a recounting or a telling of events past that are human. The human past is rooted in events but told by names. When there were no humans, there could be no history. Prior to words, and eventually writing, there was no history; only prehistory. History must have its events and its story, but that is not all. The story, the recounting, the telling must come with meaning. History is the story, the recounting, the telling of past human events *with meaning.*

The radical postmodern purist can't have a history, for she can't have historical facts. The postmodern can only have fiction. Fiction is good. It can teach us morality and beauty and value. Yet fiction's value, and hence postmodernism's value, is derivative. Meaning cannot ultimately be separated from reference. Fiction's meaning is the reflection and exposure of the empirical; it is not the empirical itself.

Neither can facts alone have meaning. For meaning there must be context. For context, there must be words or other symbol systems. When *adam* names the animals, meaning comes to be. *adam* affirms the animals, recognizes their being, lays alongside them symbols through which the world is mediated. But naming sometimes does more than affirm. It creates. *adam*'s naming creates the whole category of livestock. It makes livestock and hence livestock stand in a new relation to humans; the animals no longer roam free in nature. Some animals are stock, to

---

1. The data is not the facts either. The data is the written (and spoken, and archeological) information. The facts are, so to speak, "what actually happened." What actually happened, though, may be affected by other things. Continue on to see how this might look.

be raised, nurtured, cared for, and to stand in intimate relation to *adam*. So when *adam* names the animals, he creates at least one new category, a new kind of being. Yet God cannot find a helper, a social being with whom *adam* can have communion. The animals don't have what it takes, no matter what *adam* names them. Naming has its limitations. The naming by *adam* is in some sense a failure. Only when God does creative surgery on *adam*, taking *adam*'s rib and molding the woman does a person of *adam*'s equal come forth. And *adam* names himself after her kind—*ishshah* from *ish*. She is not an animal, she is not livestock, she is not other. The name "woman" is a symbol forever connecting the woman and the man. It is a social naming.

Historical naming is like this social naming. Historical naming connects us in our age to all those who have gone before. It is the great communion of all persons, living and dead, the recognition of our relationship to those of other ages. Abraham and Sarah carried the seeds of the nation of Israel in their bodies. We are biologically related. But when God renames Jacob ("grabs the heel") with the name of Israel ("struggles with God"), the importance of naming fairly shouts at us. By naming, people are made and a people are made. We are metaphysically, morally, and spiritually connected.[2] Historical naming—the telling, the writing, the making of history—is not the naming of fictionalization of the radical postmodern.

Fictional naming—making a world out of whole cloth—is derivative upon historical naming. When we think of our world as no more than fictional, as no more than names alone, fiction itself ceases to have power, ceases to refer, ceases to mean. The radical postmodern is a fictional creature, without reference, without meaning, for such a postmodern has no history. Hence, history, and not fiction, is primary. History is what we live.

History is lived and made. History is lived and made *by us*. "History" is ambiguous. Well should it be, for it is *us*, in all our human ambiguity. History is both history the written and spoken, and history the lived and made. Let's turn now to consider history lived and made, and its relationship to history written.

---

2. Chesterton says that true democracy is not opposed to tradition but rather opens the doors to the past and our ancestors, for true democracy gives votes to the most obscure among us. True democracy is a democracy of the dead. See Chesterton, *Orthodoxy*, 48.

What we do, what we say, what we make, what we accomplish, these are the things of historical "fact." These and these alone are the facts of history. The stories we tell of real people, of their triumphs, their failures, and their mediocracies, these are the things of history written and spoken, of meaning made. A difficulty arises here, for the "facts" upon which history written rests are *recorded*, otherwise there could be no history written. But in recording, whether in written or spoken form, we interpret. When we interpret, we name and we thereby give meaning to the "facts." What are the facts? The facts are lived. The facts are recorded. So, indeed, facts are doubly lived. They are lived and then relived in the recording. History written entails that the twice-lived facts are interpreted again and therefore lived a third time. But let's look first simply at being lived. What is it to live history, to make history? It is to act, whether well or poorly, but it is to act.

An act should be distinguished from an event. In one sense, events are purely unhuman. That is the way we think of them, at least. What we say is that events can occur without us or that prehistory occurred in objective space and time, with no human watching, thinking, or commenting. Thus events occurred long before any humans were about. But to have humans about, is to have *events* about. Another ambiguity lurks furtively here. To be "about" means to be present—to have events about is for events to exist, to occur. "About" also means to carry meaning. To have humans *about* is to have events *about* in both these senses. The aboutness of events—the meaning of events—can only occur when humans are about, for humans have aboutness. We are meaning makers, for we have purpose and intention—we have aboutness. Events become new and newly shaped when humans are about, because humans have aboutness. What of prehuman events; what are they about? They cannot be about anything. Prehuman events are just occurrences. However, to have humans about is to make events *about* something—a meaning, a truth, a story. Had we been there, in the prehuman world, could we have observed the events? Perhaps. But could we have named those events without the events being changed? We've discussed the power of the name, the symbol, to affirm. Prehistory could not, as such, be described by us and so in some sense, we couldn't have been there. Our description reorientates the world we describe. With the presence of the human, events become about something. Our affirming this or that event to talk about, to interpret, to make a story about, gives that event a meaning, a point, that it otherwise would not have.

So, possibly there were events before humans but not events we can discuss or name.[3] Any named event is an event lifted out of one kind of being into another by the lever of words. So plain or mere events we cannot know (the "prehuman"), while human events we can know because we've taken note of them, affirming them with our names. Human events as such are the facts of history. Such events are lived events. Mere events are those with which no human interacted. Once-lived events are those that humans took note of, but of which there is no written, oral, or otherwise recorded account. No history can be written of these events. Twice-lived events are the true facts of history, for they are recorded for posterity. Historical facts, then, are events—human events, twice-lived (experienced, named, and recorded). In so naming and then recording events, we act. So there are actions. But actions also come in two kinds, actions dealing with events and pure actions.

Actions are in no sense mere events, for mere events come about by sheer force of nature.[4] Actions come about by us, the human. Actions are peculiar, nonnatural occurrences. What is it to act? To act is to be human. To be human is to be free. Actions are free and not the result of blind nature.[5] Herein is the difference between mere events and actions. Mere events in no way are touched by the human and therefore we have no access to them. Herein also is the difference between mere events and human events, for human events require free interpretation, the naming of events. This naming of events changes the ontology—the being status—of mere events into human events and therefore into historical facts. Historical facts, then, are one and all interpreted, either named events or actions. The explosion of Mt. St. Helens is a named event, and therefore is *historical* fact. Named events occur at the intersection of "raw" nature and human interest. One acts when one names the explosion of Mt. St. Helens but one does not cause, pure and simple, the historical fact. But some things historical are simply human action:

3. For some related and valuable comments, see Barfield, *Saving the Appearances*, 36–39.

4. I recognize all the issues attending to the problem of humanity's relation to nonhuman nature. There is, of course, a perfectly good sense in which humans and human activities are natural, part of the created order.

5. I don't believe in "blind nature" either, since nature is created by God. But for our purposes, the contrast between blind nature and human action is useful.

the decision to stay on the mountain, as some people did, even after being warned of its explosive potential, for example. So we have historical facts rooted in event and historical facts rooted only in action. But all are named. Thus the difficulty in talking about history as facts, as if the facts exist out there, independent of human naming.[6]

Here we face more directly the paradox and challenge of history. For on the one hand we know history to be a story bordered by and beholden to historical data, the written and spoken events and actions. On the other hand, names already touch this data, affirming them as important and meaningful. History seems to hold itself up by its own proverbial bootstraps. Yet history is unlike fiction, which *completely* holds itself up by its bootstraps. Fiction need make no reference to the Real, for the fiction author can make up her facts. Historians cannot. Their facts are not events. Instead, historian's facts are concocted out of "event-stuff," stuff that influences and therefore causes the historical facts to be the way they are. But historical facts also are influenced and therefore caused by the human, the other stuff of history. The human influence of naming contributes to the *being* of historical facts. Historical facts are left mysterious, neither simply determined nor simply free. History is not, thus, suspended above the earth by its own laces, but enigmatically suspended above and yet built upon the events that we cannot access without influencing. This mystery makes history distinctive, a spider's web so large that although suspended somewhat, we can't see where the anchors attach. We can only see the middle where we live and continue to give meaning to the web. We do this both by *making* parts of it and also by *trusting* that it all connects to parts made by others and, ultimately that it is rooted in the "way things are." But the "way things are," the part we cannot see, remains shadowy.

The chapter "Fiction" notes that in radical postmodernism we mortals put ourselves above the Real, becoming fiction writers on a cosmic scale. Therein rests radical postmodernism's heresy. We don't want to settle for this extreme postmodernism anymore than does Elaine Risley. We long to occupy the space of the Real, the Solid, the Impassable. And as "Fiction" suggests, the truth lies in the mean *between* the objective (but meaningless on-its-own) world of things and the fictional (but unrooted) world of names. Truth lies in the space we call history, the space

---

6. Making the above distinctions can help us recognize why.

between objective facts—the uninterpreted and thus objective events and stuff of the "way things are"—and the make-belief of fiction.

History lies between objectivity and fiction because we humans are at its center. Humans, unlike the nonhuman natural, are richly free, and that makes all the difference. Our freedom sets us apart. Freedom makes *ishshah* and *ish* of the same kind. Freedom is the central gift given to us. For in being free, we are made capable of naming. In naming, we are capable of shaping the world by affirming some things and denying others, of cutting and molding the world the way it seems best to us.

Our freedom enables our making history, both in the writing and in the acting. When we write history, we tell a story with meaning, for history is the story, the recounting, the telling of past human events with meaning. Yet when we act, we make history. Events alone do not a history make, for history is human and requires humans for its making. History is a garden, requiring order. Ultimately only free actions are the stuff of history, for mere events cannot play a part in that history. Only interpreted events can play a part. In interpretation, events cease to be mere events and become the events of historical data. As such, they have interacted with the freedom of the human and thus become something other than they were.

Our interpreting, our naming of things, writes the history. Historian Perry Miller's *Errand into the Wilderness* is history written. It is based on historical facts, facts recorded. The recording is an action. Indeed, taking note of some event to record it involves an action. Our acting gives us something to write about. Our acting, then, is prior to writing history. Our acting makes history a thing with meaning. The meaning of history is not discovered but made by our actions. We act when we initially name historical facts either by interacting with events or by doing actions and later by recording them. Later we name as we write history. The radical postmodern claims there is nothing there to name. In naming naming as most important, the postmodern denies the very thing that gives naming its value, its rootedness in the facts of freedom. Radical postmodernism is freedom run amuck—freedom without limitations or facts, and without that mysterious objectivity in which the historian rests.

History thrives in the middle ground between objectivity—what the moderns wanted—and fiction—what the radical postmoderns revel in. Objectivity does not force the historian to leave the facts as "bare" facts. Facts are interpreted, they are "felt" facts—facts doubly and triply lived. Each historian tells a different story, makes a different world, by evaluating, emphasizing, sorting, weighing, and deciding which facts are to be presented and in what order, and with what importance. History is never fixed. The historian tells our past with both our actions and events important to those actions, and she tells this story with meaning. The historian names our past. In this naming we are free. In this freedom we have our being. Our being, in turn, is rooted in the Real.

History, unlike fiction, is open to the future because of freedom. Indeed, history is never fixed because the future is never fixed. We are free to tell and, in fact, free to retell the story of the past. Yet mysteriously, freedom is bound by the objectivity of the past, to the facts of freedom. The stumbling block becomes the cornerstone. What is this objectivity? Whence this freedom?

5

Freewill

The choices I've made in my life bring me, at least in part, to where I am. The choices of others contribute to where I am as well. Some choices are good ones. Some not so good. One term not long ago I decided to teach a course on freewill. Some helpful friends who are experts in the area pointed out some books to use for the course. The books were good ones, but really hard. Indeed, I find this whole field of philosophy to be extraordinarily difficult to grasp.

Part of the problem is that my own intuitions seem to shift whenever I think about freewill. Some days my intuitions lean toward what is traditionally called "compatibilism," where freewill is just the ability to follow one's wants and desires and where one's wants and desires are the result of the warp and woof of a deterministic universe. Acts are only unfree, on this view, when something "external" interferes with one's natural ability to follow one's desires. The ability to follow one's wants and desires is considered enough to grant one responsibility or to hold one responsible. The problem here is that if my wants and desires are determined, could I choose to do otherwise and if not, in what sense am I really responsible?

Most days I'm what is traditionally called a "libertarian," one who thinks freewill is incompatible with a deterministic take on the world, from which it follows that if we have freewill, determinism is false. That's not to say that nothing is determined but rather that human free choice can intervene in the flow of determined events. The problem here is that it seems that such a power is totally disconnected to anything else. Such acts, it is thought, are random, with no cause or source. No antecedent conditions lead up to the supposed free actions. Randomness, however, doesn't give us responsibility either. If a truly random brain event leads to my dropping a heavy weight on your toe, surely I'm not responsible.

There are those who think libertarianism is correct but mysterious. We can't really explain it, but we need it to make sense of our moral activity and judgments. At the end of the term when I taught the course on freewill, I saw myself pretty much totally leaning this way. I came to be confirmed in my view that libertarian freewill is as close as humans get to a divine-like ex nihilo creative activity. I'm happy with that. The real issue, however, is to wonder what makes someone an expert on freewill. Sure, some have studied and tried with extraordinary effort to make sense of this notion. In that sense some are experts. But in another sense, doesn't anyone of us have the chance to be a real expert at applying our freewill? What would that look like?

In the following pages, I don't try to solve the traditional problem of freewill. I won't be that presumptuous. I will say some things about how the problem is related to some of the things I've said so far. But the discussion gets thick (too thick, perhaps, for some and not thick enough, I'm sure, for the experts). So I won't mind (in fact, I'll probably never know!) if you skip this chapter. It's the most abstract in the book. Having said that, I will to go on.

The will has caused more ink to bleed out of pens and quills than, perhaps, nearly any other subject. In what sense can the will cause ink to bleed? Ink is caused to bleed because the pen or quill is upright, the ink's viscosity is set for the flowing of the ink, the ball or nib touches the paper, and gravity and air pressure do the rest. Yet this scientific explanation of flowing ink doesn't connect to the meaning of the first sentence. Rather, it is *the will* that causes bleeding ink. In what sense can the will cause a physical event, the bleeding of ink, to occur? Is the will just some other physical thing? Typically, the response to this sort of question is negative. If humans have a will, it is not physical but mental. The status of mental objects, however, is up for grabs, philosophically. I will just stipulate that the mental is not reducible to the physical, for if it is, then I believe the notion of freewill is impossible, except in the compatibilist sense that I reject. I don't see how the mental can be reduced to or so dependent upon the physical that each mental event is the inevitable result of previous physical states.

The will has caused more ink to flow than any other subject. This suggests that the will demands to be written about. This demand is not unique to the will. Lots of things demand to be written about, or demand to be done, or demand their own way. Such demands are, of course, metaphorical demands. The will isn't talking to us. There is instead a sense that the subject is so important that it needs to be written about. How so? Humans need to understand. That is our nature. When faced with such a demand, we respond willfully. Either one answers the demand affirmatively or negatively. Both require one's will. But in all cases, the will looks forward. So I reject the notion that the will is just another cause, like the pull of gravity and the physical attributes of ink leading to the ink flowing from the nib of the pen. The will, if it is a cause, is of a sort that requires a future response. That is the nature of the sorts of demands I've mentioned. The demand expects a future response. So the will's response to the demand is future oriented. The demand does not *cause* the writing in some scientific sense. Rather, the demand, if answered affirmatively, is what Aristotle called a final cause. The will must have final causes on which to work, goals to move toward. Thus, the will, to be the will, must be future oriented. Future orientation is of the utmost importance for understanding the will, for future orientation connects the will to purpose and purpose demands meaning. In our freewill we humans find our meaning. Without it, life is without point. Thus the will causes ink to bleed not in the sense of external demand or cause, but ultimately because the person who does the writing wills. Her will causes the pen to be put into touch with the paper, holds the pen upright, and so forth. She purposes to do so.

Freewill demands that we consider the consequences, that we think about the future. Freewill lays out in front of us the vastly huge number of possible paths we might pursue. The future, not having happened, is not fixed. It is bordered by limitations, however, the limitations of the natural order and the limitations of logic. Even Descartes, who thought the will unlimited, perhaps even infinite, in what it could choose, still recognized the physical limits of the world in which we live. Although I can *will* to jump to the moon, I won't be able actually to accomplish what I will, for the physical situation limits what I can *actually do*. And contrary to Descartes, most certainly I cannot will what is *logically* impossible. So willing is limited, not only in what can be willed logically, but in what the will can actually bring about, by the physical laws of the world.

Yet within these bounds, the future remains open and wildly so. Since the future is open to the will, the will is purpose and hence meaning driven. Whatever the willer takes to be important calls will into action.

We can choose a good many paths upon which to tread. We can move to Alaska, live in the wilderness, and live off the land. We can move to New York and try our hand at acting. Or we can live at home, work in the local foundry, and take care of our elderly parents. Freewill allows us to choose good and bad as well. We can steal that candy bar or leave it on the shelf, or we can learn directly from our parents that stealing is wrong. We can use the power of language to build people up, or we can use it to tear people down. We can hold people accountable to justice, or we can let the chips fall where they may. Freewill gives us a huge range of possibilities, even if they are limited in logic, on the level of the will itself, and limited in fact, on the level of implementation.

Is there a will and if so, what is its nature? I've noted the huge philosophical problem here. So large is the problem that I chose just to state my opinion without much argument. Yet one can hardly tackle the issues of history, fiction, and naming without entering the difficult valleys—or should we say mountain tops—of the will. Perhaps, though, rather than attacking the problem straight on, we can sneak up behind it by asking first why we think there is a problem with freewill in the first place. Freewill seems so obvious, why do we question its existence?

A philosophical commonplace is that the problem of freewill is generated by the fact that nature is so orderly, so law-like. The existence of the inexorable laws of nature rule out freewill. We humans, being natural, must fall under these laws and therefore are not free or are free only in the limited compatibilist sense. Since every event has a cause, and in turn, these causes are events that have causes, it is said that no event, human or natural, can be done freely. The inexorable parade of events determines each event, and no event can come about without the determined events that came before it. On march the events of causation, and out marches freewill, over the cliff of reason, into the garbage heap of meaningless notions. This is why we think there is a problem with freewill. Freewill cannot be, because there simply is no room for it in the causal web of laws and necessities.

Yet as I suggested in earlier chapters, the so-called inexorable laws of nature are not as inexorable as we are accustomed to think. Thus, the traditional way of structuring the problem of freewill is, I think, itself problematic. The "laws" of nature are not necessary. They are, as Hume so-well points out, and Chesterton so amusingly describes, radically contingent. The apple does not *have* to fall down. Whence the necessity of nature then, and why think we are not free? Since the laws of nature are not the laws of logic—that is to say, since the laws of nature are contingent—why think that even if humans do fall generally under some laws of nature that there are no exceptions to those laws? The apple does not *have* to fall down; nor do I *have* to do what my antecedent situation demands that I do. Wouldn't this automatically leave room for freewill? Perhaps, but one other issue needs settling.

With the observation that the causal web and the laws of nature are contingent, it may be suggested that freewill happens, so to speak, in the random events that *might possibly* or perhaps even *do* occur between the laws of nature—that is, where the laws of nature meet their limits. Call this the "middle road solution." But caution is called for here. For an event to be random means that it has no antecedent events causally leading up to it. Such an event is, so to speak, without cause or reason; it is an event from nowhere and nothing. This won't give us freewill.

Some people think that if the laws of nature are not completely deterministic—that is, if some events are random, without cause or reason—that the world would be chaotic. This isn't so. All the events could be ordered by determinism except for one or two and the world would still be quite orderly. Let's nevertheless take the worse case, and assume that all events are random, that is, that none have prior events leading up to them at all. Can this help freewill? No. In a truly random universe, no event would have a reason for happening. When an event has no cause or reason, nothing or no one is responsible for it. How could I (or anyone) be responsible for an action that had no cause or reason and that, *a forteriori*, I didn't do? One thing we know is that free actions are actions attended by responsibility. Responsibility brings with it the need for things happening according to some reason or other. Some connection must exist between the actor and the action. If the "action" is purely random, there is no antecedent connection. Thus there is no true action at all. So while determinism doesn't follow from the laws of nature, freewill doesn't follow from some kind of total randomness either. So what about the "middle road solution?" What if the world is determined in all but for a few random events? Can freewill happen in the random spaces? No, for then everything is either determined or random, and neither one provides for freewill of the sort I'm concerned with, libertarian freewill. Determined events are not forward looking and random events are not the type of thing for which we can be responsible.

We were trying to sneak up behind the issue of whether we have freewill by looking at why we think there is a problem with freewill. Why is there a problem with freewill? I believe there is no real problem, at least as typically considered. If the world's events were completely determined, because the laws of nature are necessary, then there is no room for freewill. But the laws of nature are contingent and therefore freewill is not ruled out by their existence. There is no problem theoretically for freewill, since determinism isn't very firmly rooted. Is there a problem on the other end? If there were no deterministic web, are the remaining events free? Well, there might be a problem if the only possibility for other events were randomness. If the defender of freewill hides in the possible randomness of some events, the responsibility for free events disappears in the randomness. Random events do not occur for a reason. Such events cannot be "done" by anyone. These events are not, thus, free. But is it even worth considering random events as the space for freewill? We are not very happy with the idea of randomness. To say *no* event has a prior cause would make the orderliness of the world a very odd and difficult-to-explain fact. Perhaps some events are random. So long as not many are, the orderliness of the world remains intact. But must all events be either determined or random? Why can't there be free events, that is, events that are done for a (future) reason, not fixed, not determined, and yet not random? The idea is not incoherent, and there appears to be logical space for free events. But making a logical space for such events does not leave us with an account of freewill or an argument for it.

In "History" I spoke of the facts of freedom—the facts in virtue of which freewill is possible. These, it might be thought, are facts resulting simply from the inexorable march of the so-called laws of nature. As such, one might think of the facts of freedom as being driven from "behind," since certain events have occurred, and the laws of nature simply force one from event A to event B. But that is overly simple. To understand the facts of freedom more clearly, let us look again at the facts of fiction.

In fiction, the empirical facts are made up and they are in no way determined by the laws of nature operating outside the fiction, although fiction remains bound by the laws of logic. Yet once the facts are fixed in a fictional work, the work cannot be changed, and neither can any of the events or properties attached to the fictional characters. No fictional character *really* chooses what to wear or where to live or how to get there, although the author may portray the events as involving choice. There is no openness to the future, there is no freewill. Fictional characters do not choose what to do—they are not free. That they lack freewill, however, does not derive from a determined or fixed natural order from "behind," for we know that these fictional characters need not fall under the laws of nature.

Whence comes this fixity of fictional characters, if not from the necessity of following the laws of nature? One must look elsewhere. Any fixity of fictional characters is due not to the laws of nature but to the author. The author, of course, hovers outside the novel and whatever rules it follows. In the novel, the laws of nature by which the author standardly lives—lives by in real life—are suspended. In suspending these laws in the novel, the past is suspended and, along with it, the future. The novel is timeless. Hence, no openness to the future exists for fictional creatures and because of this, there is no freewill. The future, as well as the past, is fixed. This fixity rules out freewill. But we now know that fixity is not necessarily natural determinism. Fixity can be something other than determinism.

We also know that a *lack* of fixity does not suffice for freewill, for random events are not fixed and yet neither can they be free. Nor is freewill simply a lack of determinism, for fictional characters are not determined by the laws of nature and yet they are not free. So freewill is neither random nor determined nor fixed. Instead, freewill is a positive force, an ability, a power. Randomness brings nothing positive to allow for freewill. The falsity of determinism brings nothing positive to explain freewill. Neither does a mere lack of fixity bring freewill. Freewill and lack of fixity are not the same thing. On the other hand, there is a connection between the lack of freewill and the fixity of fictional events. But is it the fictional necessity that denies the characters freewill or is it the lack of freewill that creates the necessity of the fictional creatures? I believe the lack of freewill is prior to the fixity of the fictional events. Without freewill, and because randomness won't explain order, fixity follows. Fixity occurs because of the freewill of the author—someone outside the story altogether—and the metaphysical "thinness" of fictional creatures. Such thin creatures don't have will.

What about real life? If we lacked freewill, would our lives be fixed like fiction? Of course, our lives wouldn't be fixed from "behind," for that requires the necessity of the laws of nature. Any fixity would come, so to speak, *from outside the story*. Such fixity would be much more horrendous than anything brought about by the so-called laws of nature. Our lives would be laid down, step by step, move by move, and we would be no more than fictional creatures, controlled by some manipulative author. But do we have an author? Here we come to the issue of why there is a world at all, if the laws are contingent. It is natural to suggest that the world is because God made it to be so. Perhaps God is the source of unfreedom, an ultimate authorial manipulator.

One might suppose that God is such a source, but what motivation is there for that? Well, we have seen that, contrary to the problem of freewill being rooted in the so-called "necessity" of the contingent laws of nature, the problem of freewill may be rooted elsewhere. Fictional characters are unfree precisely because they are *not* bound by the laws of nature and yet they are fixed. They exist, but the laws of nature do not apply to them and therefore the source of their unfreedom is something else. In fact, their *very being* must come from something else. In order for fictional creatures to come to be, there must be some outside, creative force—the author. Since fictional creatures are not bound by any law of nature, whence comes their being? In order to have being at all, there must be some creator, a creator who, in the case of fictional characters, pulls all the strings, leaving the fictional character with no freewill. The fictional character has no being independent of the story being told.

In contrast, real humans are free even though bounded by the laws of nature, laws that are neither random nor completely determined. What we learn from fiction is that if fictional beings are to exist at all, and since they are in no way bound by the laws of nature, they must have a creator. So for us humans. Although we are bound in some ways by the laws of nature, we don't have to be the way we are—nature is contingent—and the world is not as deterministic as its orderliness might suggest. Why, then, do we exist? We too, must have a creator. But is this creator a divine author who makes sure things come out the way God wants them to, a divine novelist? If so, God becomes a source of fixity and unfreedom for us, just as the author of a novel is the source of the fictional character's unfreedom. Such is a cruel world, a world without meaning. But we are not fictional creatures, for the laws of nature apply to us. Thus, we suspect that our status is different from the fixity of the fictional. We live under the facts of freedom rather than the facts of fiction. We have freewill.

If God is not a novelist, what is the alternative? What if we start with the idea that God authors our lives, but does not sit at an ontological distance and force us to act according to whatever comes from the divine pen? Such an author need not write us like the fiction in a novel or fairy tale. Perhaps God is more like a playwright who writes the basic story, and suggests some lines, but who leaves it up to the actors to develop.[1] Some fixity exists here (the basic limitations of the story and the story line) but there is also freewill (the interpretation by the actor and the director). In fact, it is because of the nature of the play, designed as a play, that not everything is fixed and the final outcome is up to the actor *combined with* the author rather than just the author. Likewise, it is because of the nature of the universe, designed with actors, that not everything is fixed and the final outcome is up to the actors *combined with* the author rather than just the author himself. We as actors freely interpret and deal with whatever is thrown at us. Further, just as the playwright and the directors and actors are all persons, so are God and the human actors all persons. Is God a fiction writer who fixes our every step? Perhaps, but there appears to be no particularly good reason to think so. What fixity we have seems to come from behind rather than above, so why not choose the other possibility, namely that God made us free? With God as playwright, rather than novelist, at least the possibility of freewill exists. Why doesn't God fix our every step like the author of a novel, and make us unfree? That is a mystery no less deep than freewill itself, but perhaps God makes us free simply because God can, unlike the human novelist and her characters.

The laws of nature explain in part why we are the way we are. Were it not for the laws of nature, we would not be anything other than fictional creatures for we would not have a history. This latter is the fate of fictional creatures. Without the laws of nature, we would be mere fictions, without true reality and, therefore, without freewill. In fiction, the laws of nature are suspendable, and so we can have people in fairy tales living through horrendous things and still being granted new lives altogether. Yet there is reason to think we are not in fiction pure and simple but perhaps in a play. There is historicity to a play, when it is performed—

---

1. See some comments of Sayers, *Mind of the Maker*, 61–84.

that is, there are *real* people acting. We are historical people, not strictly fictional, and hence the laws of nature are not totally suspendable for us. We cannot, in the sense of the fairy tale hero, receive a new life altogether. The laws instead allow us to have some small independence of being, to interpret what is happening, to read our lines *our* way. The egg and sperm unite, and the laws of nature take their course. These facts of our freedom are confusedly taken by the determinist to be the very laws of nature that force a lack of freewill for humans. On the contrary, freewill is impossible *without* the laws of nature, the very things that are beyond our freewill, for without them we would not be historical creatures and hence not have a future, the terrain of freedom. Without freewill, we would slip into fictionality. We are not creatures of fiction but creatures of history. Therefore the limits to our freewill are found in the mysterious stuff over which neither the historian nor the historical person has control: the laws of nature and what we might call "the Real." But what is this freewill, this positive force, this ability to choose? It requires a number of things, including a certain view of the person and, it seems, a certain view of God. Otherwise, we get randomness instead of freewill. But some other things can be said of freewill itself.

"Freedom," Eric Gill says, "is not incompatible with discipline, it is only incompatible with irresponsibility."[2] Discipline we have, at least in part, by the laws of nature. We are disciplined by the order of the world, for we cannot jump to the moon. We cannot jump to the moon not because we cannot will it, but because we do not have the physical ability to follow through with our willful choice. Discipline, as Eric Gill means it, of course, is probably not the external kind of discipline of the "ways things are" but rather a kind of choice we make to follow the rules. Gill most likely has in mind following the laws of human behavior rather than following the laws of nature. But why stop at the laws of behavior? Why not take the laws of nature as a source of discipline? A child is disciplined in learning to walk by the hard nature of the floor and the pull of gravity. An athlete is disciplined by the height of the bar over which she is to jump. Both choose discipline when they get up and try again. Without the boundaries of nature and the laws embedded therein, all would be random, discipline impossible, and freewill beyond our power. Discipline is central to freewill. So is responsibility, which Gill captures by saying freewill is only incompatible with irresponsibility.

2. Gill, "First Things," 40.

True freewill is responsible. Here I echo St. Augustine. Where I am not responsible, I am not truly free. We find two ways in which I might not be responsible. First, I might be irresponsible by choosing the wrong thing, the wrong path, the wrong direction. That is, I have the capacity to choose well, but fail to do so. But surely it is *because* we are free that we can be held responsible for such actions. Thus understood, perhaps we should read Gill as saying that freewill is not consistent with *non*responsibility. But this is not what Gill says. He says freewill is inconsistent with *ir*responsibility. Being irresponsible is not the same as being nonresponsible. Responsible and nonresponsible are the truly logical incompatibles. Responsibility and irresponsibility are not truly logically incompatible. In fact, one cannot be irresponsible without *being* responsible! One acts irresponsibly when one doesn't pay sufficient attention to one's responsibility or when one simply decides to ignore one's responsibility. To be responsible is to have the capacity to act responsibly (to act well) *and* the capacity to act irresponsibly (to act poorly). So to be free is to be responsible. But to be irresponsible is also to be responsible. So how can being free be incompatible, as Gill says, with irresponsibility?

Perhaps all Gill means is that freewill is abused when one is irresponsible, and in this sense, freewill is incompatible with irresponsibility. One uses the gift of freewill to do what freewill gives one the power *to avoid*. So being free is something more than merely *the capacity* to act well or badly. Both responsibility and irresponsibility are incompatible with fixity, for in fixity one can neither act well nor act poorly, one can neither act responsibly nor act irresponsibly, since one cannot *act* at all. Freewill, thus being required for responsibility *and* irresponsibility, is required for action. True freewill is what makes us actors. True freewill is therefore what makes us human. True freewill is real responsibility; it is the ability to act well. To be free is to be responsible. So freewill is incompatible with irresponsibility because true freewill is the ability to act well, and to act irresponsibly is to act poorly. So the ability to act (freewill) is incompatible with acting poorly (irresponsibility). When we act poorly, when we act irresponsibly, we act contrary to our true freewill. Irresponsibility is derivative from responsibility. True freewill is responsibility in the fullest sense of the word. When we act irresponsibly, we act in a less than fully human way; we become slaves to wrongness, to irresponsibility.

True freewill is not incompatible with discipline, whether it is the discipline of nature or the discipline of character. Without freewill, in fact, there could be no discipline of either sort. Begin with character. Our characters can only be improved if we are free. In fact, we can only *have* a character if we are free. In order to develop character, I must choose to do good things. I cannot choose to do good things, if I am only fictional, made up entirely by someone else. Nor can the discipline of nature be discipline, unless I have freewill. I can only choose to get up off the floor after having fallen down, or choose to try the high jump again, after failing to clear the bar, if I am free. Discipline is not only consistent with freewill; discipline requires freewill, as freewill requires discipline.

Thus, the laws of nature, in some sense, allow us to be free, for without the laws of nature, we would not be historical but fictional. The facts of freedom enable our freewill, and they make us historical rather than fictional creatures. History, unlike fiction, is open to the future. Indeed, history is never fixed because the future is never fixed, except when the forces of determinism are in play and controlling. But they are not totally so, as we know from Hume's teaching. So we are free to tell, and in fact, free to retell, the story of the past because the future is not totally determined. When we tell and retell the past, however, we remain bound by the historical facts, much in the way our free choices aimed toward the future are bound by the laws of nature. Yet just as there are many ways of telling the story of the past, so there are many ways of living our lives. History made, as opposed to history written, is a life lived. We make history as we live. But life lived also merges with history written. Just as the historian chooses what facts to report and interpret, how to order those facts, and how to interpret those facts, so the person living her or his life chooses what facts to use and interpret, what order to present them in, how to interpret them, and what disciplines to follow. On these bases, she or he makes the decisions that send the person off in one direction rather than another. Our free choices in life are the free choices not just of the actor in history, but of the historian writing history. Where history written and life lived merge together, then, is on the plane of history made. Our lives are history made, and it is freewill that makes this possible.

History has been defined as the story, the recounting, the telling of past human events *with meaning*. Left on the level of chronology, history is no more than a string of contextless, and therefore meaningless, events. Likewise, left on the level of mere events, our lives are no more than pointless, meaningless, strings of occurrences. But written history is the telling of the past with meaning. The meaning comes from the story-telling power of the human. The creative, freely interpretive skill of the historian is absolutely essential to the writing of history. Likewise, real living is the living of our stories with meaning. Our lives—our stories, if you will—are the results of the creative, freely interpretive skill of the person living his or her life. For this, we need freewill. It is in freedom that our meaning is possible.

Freewill, then, is the extension of these two things: The disciplines of nature, over which we have no control but which keep us from total fictionalizing, and the disciplines of meaning making, in which we have to create our own stories. But we are not alone. If we are left with nature alone as a source of freewill, we can explain neither freewill nor why we are at all. There must be an Author, a Great Historian, who posits the facts of freedom (as connected to the laws of nature) and hence contrasts us with merely fictional creatures. God, thus understood, becomes central to the story. But were the divine merely writing fiction, God would be making up all the facts and making all the choices, and we would not be historical. God is writing history, and God too, as historical, is bound by the facts (once they are facts) in a mysterious way. But just as when humans write history, and all the facts are made meaningful by the human interpreter, the divine, too, makes all the facts meaningful. God does this in the context of a divine set of limitations. God's limitation is our freewill. For not even God can make us free and then force us to operate in a controlled way. Although the laws of nature are determined by God, our freewill choices are not. God, too, must make meaning of our choices, good or ill.

6

Persons

My younger son has just turned three at this writing. He is a sensitive soul, aware of things many of the rest of us just take in stride. For example, the security building on the campus where I teach was once a residence, circa 1920, but Victorian in inspiration. It is surrounded, however, by two newer buildings. One has an addition from three years ago. It is called the Hoover building, after Hebert Hoover who attended school here as a boy, and lived a few blocks away. The other is about eight years old, an environmentally sensitive, award-winning administration-classroom building. My son Micah noticed the difference among the buildings the other day, reporting in his three-year-old's analysis that the security building "doesn't belong here."

Micah is very aware of his environment and is so sensitive, in fact, that for many months now he has chosen, quite adamantly, not to enter the toy section at the local grocery/department store. The issue isn't the toys in general, although being a sensitive soul (and bless his heart for making his parent's life easier!) he doesn't like any toys that have flashing lights and make loud noises, effectively ruling out ninety percent of today's toys. The specific issue, however, is the dolls. The first time his mother and I took him down the doll aisle, he cried and screamed as if in agony. At first we couldn't figure it out. Then we realized that he knew these dolls were not real people but some sort of "wanna be" people. He knew they looked real (have you seen how life-like today's dolls are?) but also sensed, like the security building, that they didn't belong with the rest of us real people. These dolls may walk, wriggle, pee, poop, close their eyes when they sleep, wink when they don't, and even talk. But my son, at just over a year, knew that the appropriate response is to get away from these horrors of high technology! It made me wonder about what we are doing to the real people of whom we think far less than ourselves. They are not, in our minds, just "a little lower than the angels" but perhaps like Descartes' automatons, now fashioned by the modern techno-mechanical-industrial world we've created.

People are essentially free. Without freedom, the human cannot be, for to be human is to act, and to act is to be free. But I don't want to overemphasize this freedom. To simply define humans as beings who act, to say that the human being is really the human doing, is to leave the human person on the level of a Sartrean freedom. Sartre says humanity is "condemned to be free."[1] In contrast, Gabriel Marcel notes, if one is to take the notion of being condemned to be free seriously, one must see freedom as a loss, a deprivation.[2] A condemnation requires something to be removed. For Sartre, freedom is a deprivation. Freedom is not a gift, a positive force, a power to do creative things. It is a condemnation, a denial, a taking away, even though Sartre attempts to have freedom be both a deprivation *and* a creative power.[3]

To leave the human person as simply someone who *does* rather than as someone who *is*, leaves the human person wildly and absolutely free. Sartre would have us create ourselves, to grant ourselves our own being, our own essence. To do so leaves us alone, without explanation, without a connection to a reality other than the one we create. To think that we can create ourselves out of whole cloth is the heresy of the Garden of Eden. It is naming without limits. Free we are; free we are and wildly so. But we are not absolutely free. Absolute freedom destroys us. Sartre thus foreshadows the radical postmodern.

Freedom is rooted in our being, in what we are. What we are is the image of God. We are tempted to think of the image of God as we might think of fictional characters who are made strictly in the image of their authors. But this would be something less than flattering to God.

---

1. Sartre, *Nausea*.
2. Marcel, *Philosophy of Existentialism*, 78.
3. See Sartre, "Existentialism is Humanism," in which Sartre defends the notion the humans are free to create their own essences and yet, not having any essence, they cannot be free.

Fictional characters who are just like their authors, and decidedly so, tend not to be flattering but flat.[4] Such beings cannot provide an image of freedom. If we are God's image, we must be creative.[5] We must be able to strike out on our own. We must be able to make new worlds. So God gives us the power of the name. With naming we become something other than God, and no mere puppets. To be human is to act, but it is to act creatively.

To be creative is to be open to the future. Humans are essentially open to the future. Yet we live through the past and we live in the present. Our past connects us to others, and those others are connected to yet others, our being passed down, generation to generation. We sit around ancient fires, telling tales of how the world began, how humans were mixed out of earth and breath, how the trees popped into existence one afternoon, how we once walked with God, and how God once held our hands. Our being is rooted in the stories of our past. To treat our being as merely biological, chemical, or physical is to leave out the meaning. To leave out the meaning is to leave out what is special about us. To be *just* like God, to be *just* the same way the divine is, is to be nothing other than an exact simulacrum. But we are not fake gods, moving only the way God moves. We can think new thoughts, paint new paintings, dance new dances, and rebel new rebellions. Yet there is nothing new under the sun.

Creativity builds on the past. It always builds with the materials at hand. We cannot create *ex nihilo*; we cannot create from nothing. Even fiction is derivative.[6] The stuff of the sculpture is the stuff of the earth. The stuff of the play is the stuff of our emotions. The stuff of the essay is the stuff of our minds. Robert Nozick observes this about our bodily connection to the earth: "Eating is an intimate relationship. We place pieces of external reality inside ourselves; we swallow them more deeply inside, where they are incorporated into our own stuff, our own bodily being of flesh and blood. It is a remarkable fact that we turn parts of external reality into our own substance. We are least separate from the world in eating. The world enters into us; it becomes us. We are constituted by

---

4. See again Sayers, *Mind of the Maker*, 61–84.

5. Sayers says that the only feature of God pointed to in the Genesis creation story is God as Creator. As such, she says, we must take the image of God to be creativity, at least in the first instance.

6. Despite what Dorothy Sayers says. See Sayers, *Mind of the Maker*, 27–31.

portions of the world."[7] In the building of our bodies, the dance of the biological world, we are most closely connected to the limits of the world. Yet this physicality, this earthiness, is not just biological. It is part of our creative beings as well.

We come from the humus. Our physical and chemical makeup is continuous with and contiguous to the earth. In the story of the Garden, when the divine kneels to make *adam*, God scrapes together the dust of the earth, breathes into the dirt hot, holy breath, and a living soul is made. Wendell Berry points out that we tend to read this passage dualistically. We tend to superimpose our post-Platonic notion of body + soul = human onto what is fundamentally not a dualistic understanding of humanity. The passage really communicates a nondualistic dirt + breath = living soul understanding of humanity.[8] The soul—the thing we think most closely is our essential selves—is made up of the dirt and the holy breath of God, the divine self. Hence we have the difficulty of talking about the mind or our soulish selves without also pointing to our very fleshly bodies.

The soul is not, on this understanding, separable from the body. Yet the body itself is not the soul. Dead human bodies are not living souls. Dead bodies are no more than dirt. So the soul is, arguably, an emergent thing. Common table salt emerges out of sodium and chlorine, neither of which is good, separately, for us to consume. Yet table salt we need for health (in small amounts!). Salt has emergent properties. Like this, our souls emerge from dirt and holy breath. This emergent thing is creative and free, not wholly bound by the rules of dirt and humus. This soulish thing Plato knew was *not* identical to ultimate reality, yet enough *like* ultimate reality that it could dwell among the forms in eternal bliss.[9]

The soul is like the Creator *and* like the dirt in its soulishness. The image of God in us, the image that *is* us, the creativity we share, emerges from the holied humus. Our being is shared. The creativity is not just like God's, but different. It is human creativity and not divine creativity. As human, creativity is rooted in the physicality of the world, the created order. Yet the creativity is immense and fascinating. The worlds created by writers, painters, sculptors, chemists, physicists, and, indeed, all of us, are immensely divergent. The Aristotelian philosopher who sees the

---

7. Nozick, *Examined Life*, 55, 56.
8. Berry, "Christianity and the Survival of Creation."
9. See the arguments in Plato, *Phaedo*, where he defends the immortality of the soul.

world as made up of fundamentally fixed substances lives in a world quite unlike that proposed by the Whiteheadian philosopher of creative moments. The Calvinist theologian who views the world as one in which God's providence is overwhelming as it calls us into relationship with the divine lives in a world unlike the Arminian theologian who suggests that we do something to create a good relationship with God. The historian who tells a Marxist story of slavery in America lives in a world other than that of the classical libertarian political historian.

Yet the mystery of the world, the objective features of the reality to which we bring meaning in telling our stories, grounds all this creativity. And ultimately God roots the creativity of humanity in the divine gift of freedom, that wonderful openness to the future. God made us so open to the future that we created a whole new category for ourselves. We named ourselves sinners.

Perhaps we'd like to blame the creation of sin on someone else: Satan, maybe. But surely not. Sin is a purely human invention. The sin of the devils, whatever they may be, is of a different kind than ours, for the devils are not human. Our sin, the sin of humanity, is ours and ours alone. In fact, sin is perhaps the only thing we can truly call our own. In our creative moment of darkness, in a corner wherein we hid our shame, we mixed a nasty brew of power and evil, of treachery and deceit, the likes of which the world had never seen. No mere immorality is sin. Sin is much bigger than a few moral missteps. Sin is an ontological category. When we named ourselves sinners, we used our power of naming in both its creative and its annihilating modes.

A long history understands evil (which may not be exactly the same as sin, although sin certainly is related to evil) as a privation, a negation, an undoing of the good. Yet such an Augustinian move leaves many of us uncomfortable, perhaps not fully recognizing the "positive" aspects of evil. Surely, we say, evil is real. Certainly no one rationally denies the power of evil, its influence in the world. So we need to capture both the tradition that notes the nonbeing of evil (its meontic status) and the tradition that notes its reality. Is evil a reality with a tendency toward nonbeing? Naming ourselves sinners seems to admit of our self-destruction. We affirm the presence and power of sin when we name ourselves sinners, but we also set ourselves on the path of annihilation.

Sin is a limitation on our nature. Unlike the limitations of the humus, however, the limitation of sin is not natural to us. That is, it was not created by God. Our natural state—perhaps "true state" would be better—is the image of God untarnished: pure creativity. That is the way God made us. Yet creativity can go awry.

Exactly how we became sinners is a complex matter. Exactly what sin is, is a complex matter. Part of the story is this. The tree in the Garden, the tree of which *adam* is not to eat, is the tree of the *knowledge* of good and evil. It is neither the tree of knowledge nor the tree of good and evil. So *adam* can know things before he eats the fruit. And when *adam* eats of that fruit, he knows full well that he is not to eat of it. He is told by God. Yet what kind of knowing is this? What kind of action is *adam*'s action? He cannot know the action is evil. Hence, he cannot be doing anything morally wrong, for to accomplish a moral wrong it seems clear enough that he must have some sense of right and wrong, of good and evil. Yet *adam* doesn't have that kind of knowledge, for the tree is the tree of the knowledge of good and evil. So what kind of command is this command God gives *adam*? The command is like one a parent gives to a very young child. Don't go into the street without me! The child, not yet knowing good and evil, still may understand the command. Yet the command is not a moral one. It is a "raw" command. Just do what I say. You are too young yet to understand.

So with *adam*. Don't eat the fruit off that tree, *adam*! But *adam* knows not what evil is. He knows not what havoc and horror will be unleashed into the world by this disobedience.[10] So the disobedience is not an immorality. It is, rather, a disobedience born of ignorance. It is a disobedience born out of a mismatching of curiosity (and its sister, creativity) and finite being.[11] Our desire to know oversteps our ability to bear what we find out. God, being infinite, can know what evil is, without getting entangled in the experience of evil. Humans cannot. It is in our deed that we are undone. Our deed plunges us into the depths of darkness we could neither foresee nor understand. Our deed creates an experiential knowing of evil. Whence, then, sin? Is sin simply knowing evil?

10. Marilyn McCord Adams makes some wonderfully powerful comments about the role of our ontology in evil, as well as some equally powerful comments about the nature of what *adam* knew. See Adams, "Sin as Uncleanness," and "Theodicy without Blame."

11. There are two streams of thought on the nature of sin in Christianity. One is the Augustinian inspired notion that humans lived in a morally perfect universe from which we fell. The other is inspired more by Irenaeus where humans were more like children in the Garden of Eden. I obviously favor the latter.

Sin emerges from our creativity, our wills overstepping the bounds of our ability to handle the knowledge. Sin arises when our attempts to know overstep our being: infinite will, finite being. Although sin need not have happened, it could and did. Sin is not necessary—and yet we are all sinners. Neither is sin, in the first instance, an immorality. It is not even primarily moral (although no one can deny that immorality is sin). But sin is a part of our being, our fallen being. Sin is a corruption of the being of the holied humus. We turned our creativity upon ourselves. Sin is not trusting God, but instead, putting ourselves in God's place, knowing good and evil. The nature of sin, however, is not just a doing but a being. Sin is the knowing of good and evil by experience and by so knowing evil, we do evil. When Socrates said that to know the good is to do the good, he overlooked the other side. To know the evil is to do the evil, something no Greek philosopher would have admitted. Evil, in the Greek mind, was irrational. But then, so are we humans. To know the evil is to do the evil connects our knowing creativity with the reality and nonbeing of evil. Humans are, indeed, sinners. We are sinners, our being tending toward nonbeing, our creativity turning upon itself.

Sinners we are, but not sinners alone. We are the image of the divine as well. Our holied humus is soiled humus, true enough. The truth about the human experience is that we know both sides. To deny one at the expense of the other is to be unrealistic in our self-descriptions; it is to fall into heresy.

Dorothy Sayers, in *The Mind of the Maker*, unveils the ancient creeds of the Church by taking the creativity metaphor seriously and spelling out various doctrines in terms of the human creative act and all its varied manifestations. Her primary example, however, is fiction and literature more broadly construed. In her chapter on the incarnation, she makes a fascinating move. Throughout her book, she talks of novels and plays. All of a sudden, she shifts to explaining the Incarnation of God's divine self as "God's autobiography." Autobiography is not fiction. It is history. This is no mere quirk of her writing, an accidental slip from fiction to nonfiction. It is, rather, absolutely essential. For God is historical, just as we are. It would be heresy to think of God strictly in terms of fiction. Just as heretical is the thought that God is some distant objectivity. God is, rather, historical.[12]

---

12. And of course here I don't mean merely historical.

So are we humans. Here it is fitting to note another comment of Sayers: "But the writing of autobiography is a dangerous business; it is a mark either of great insensitiveness to danger or of an almost supernatural courage. Nobody but a god can pass unscathed through the searching ordeal of incarnation."[13] In our natures we are creative, the very image of God. We use that creativity to name ourselves sinners. In our autobiographies, we approach a self-revelation that cannot leave us unscathed. Only God can write the perfect autobiography. Our attempts will be tainted by the dark side of our soul.

---

13. Sayers, *Mind of the Maker*, 92.

7

Heresy

When I was a young and brash assistant professor I was accused of heresy. I don't recall the word being used explicitly, but it was clear that my accusers were thinking that I was not orthodox. The context for this challenge was my alma mater, an academically solid evangelical Christian college where I had returned to teach on a multi-year contract. Lest the reader think accusations of heresy only occur in such "backwater" places as Christian institutions, I've seen heresy accusations in secular academe as well. Heresy is not just a religious concept, even if its clearest roots are religious.

Let me speak to my own experience. I was teaching introduction to philosophy when a number of students, all first year men, as it turned out, decided to test me instead of me them. During the last week of class, I started to receive a number of theological questions. I soon realized that the students had organized this ahead of time and that they were taking me down through the doctrinal statement of the college to see how much of it I "actually and personally" held. When I realized this, I was not only angry but hurt (a combination of emotions that I now recognize as often confused in my soul, the former typically masking the latter). So I started to say the most liberal thing I could think of that was consistent with the school's divining rod of truth.

It was not my finest moment, for I had taken on the maturity of the young men in front of me. I'm now ashamed of my response. But it was what it was. Afterward, the students went to the president and the dean of the college. Over the course of the next several months I had a number of "talks" with the president, most of which weren't about my "heresy" but more about how great these student leaders were. I found most of these "talks" insulting. I've since been to confession over my terrible attitude toward the then president of that particular institution. The dean, I think wisely, sent the students back to speak with me individually rather than try to handle the issue from on high. The issue became such a big deal that I even heard a rumor that a nationally broadcast Christian radio commentator noted that the college had an atheistic philosophy professor. That would be me. Except not only wasn't I an atheist, no one in authority had bothered to ask me what I really thought, at least not early on. When I was finally asked (by a variety of people from the Parent's Council to trustees to students to other faculty members), I was able to show myself orthodox, enough so that I ended up staying five years.

Was I promoting heresy? I thought I was teaching. I now hope I'm wiser in how I teach. But I still rankle the theological sensibilities of my students sometimes, enough so that I get calls from parents who want to know what is going on in my classes. Now I don't think I hold to heresy. In fact, I often tell my students that I'm probably more orthodox than they typically are, because I actually know what's in the historical creeds and affirm them. Yet my experiences from the past are painful, and I wish not that the issue hadn't arisen but that we had all handled it differently.

No one much likes the word "heresy" anymore. It reeks of burnt human flesh. Yet it is a perfectly good word. It does work other words simply won't do. A few of its near relatives capture something of the same meaning, but not all. Take "dissenting view." The phrase certainly captures the notion of disagreement at the core of heresy, but one can hold a dissenting view in many discussions and yet not thereby be heretical. What of "nonconformity?" The word conveys not acting, and hence not believing, the way others do. Yet one can certainly act in a nonconforming way without thereby being heretical.

The closest words are "heterodox" and "unorthodox." Both these terms relate to opinion or belief: the first, of differing opinion or belief, the second, of belief that fails to be correct. Thus, both terms call attention to the relationship of heresy to orthodoxy. Heresy can exist only if there is orthodoxy. To be orthodox is to have right opinion. Heresy, then, is wrong opinion. But what sense of "wrong" is this? Could we just substitute "false" for "heresy?" No. To have a false opinion is to have an opinion the denial of which is true. But the denial of heresy is not just a true opinion. The denial of a heretical opinion may be an orthodox opinion, but maybe not. Orthodoxy trucks with more than just truth.

Heresy is wrong opinion. But its wrongness lies in more than just its falsity. Its wrongness lies in part in its ability to disguise the truth, to make the orthodox seem unpalatable. But there is a great deal of rationality in heresy. People down through the ages used their God-given talents to reason to heresy. This is not surprising and quite to be expected, if Chesterton is right. He says that "[t]he real trouble with this world of ours is not that it is an unreasonable world, nor even that it is a reasonable one. The commonest kind of trouble is that it is nearly reasonable, but not quite."[1] Heresy seems always to leave something out because the world is not quite reasonable. But in leaving something out, the system is made more coherent.

We like coherence. We like things to be nice and smooth. But we all know in our gut, if not in thought, that reality isn't always smooth, and it definitely isn't nice. Chesterton notes, rightly so, that heresy occurs when one thing or another is emphasized above the remaining things. That is why radical postmodernism is a heresy. It's not that radical postmodernism's claims are false in their entirety. Rather, it simply ignores certain aspects of our experience. From the difficulties we face in gaining or explaining knowledge, radical postmodernism concludes that there is no Reality. In a sense, radical postmodernism isn't the *denial* of the Real but the *ignoring* of the Real. It is the obstinacy of the Real, along with the perennial story-nature of our lives, that make up orthodoxy. The meeting of these two horizons is history. Our historicity is ultimately denied by the postmodern, just as the postmodern denies our individual realities. We are socially constructed, says the postmodern. But here another heresy creeps forward, for to say that we are socially constructed is only part of the truth. We *are* socially constructed—by God, and partly by other selves. We live embedded in a social structure, a structure centrally important to orthodoxy. Orthodoxy is a community structure. The heresy must start within the family. Leaving the family is not just heresy. That is apostasy, desertion. So orthodoxy is socially rooted, and it has social reality. So is heresy socially rooted and it, too, has a social reality.

---

1. Chesterton, *Orthodoxy*, 81.

Orthodoxy is thus historical and social. So heresy cannot be simply identified with falsity. Orthodoxy is a living, breathing, growing community of people and their beliefs, rooted in the past, looking to the future, lived in the present. As history unfolds, so does the work of God. Heresy, then, is anti-historical and, ultimately, anti-social. On the one hand, it leaves the Real unmoved and unmoving. Or, on the other hand, it leaves the Real in constant flux. In short, it leaves out the historicity of the truth, or overemphasizes it. The truth is neither some unaffected Reality, an Aristotelian unmoved mover, nor is it so embedded in change that it becomes fiction rather than history. Orthodoxy is historical, recognizing the challenge of change and the firmness of the fixed. Orthodoxy, like history, must be rewritten every generation. The truth must be re-presented. Orthodoxy does not deny the truth, nor does it deny changes in culture. It simply recognizes its own living nature.

Orthodoxy is alive because it is social. To have orthodoxy, a group of believers must exist. That group influences and is influenced by the orthodox. So, orthodoxy is right opinion in a social context. So then heresy too, must be in a social context. Heresy is not just false opinion. The word "opinion" has roots in an old word for "to think." Heresy is, then, false thinking. Some old words for taking or grasping belong to the history of the term "heresy." Heresy is the grasping, the taking, the thinking that is false. Taken all together, heresy is a false way of living, a false way of being in community. As someone thinks, so is that person. Furthermore, we could always take orthodoxy to be right belief, and not merely right opinion. But the word "believe" has very ancient roots in the notion of love or desire. To believe is to bring about, to fulfill love or desire. Thus orthodoxy is right loving. Heresy, then, would be wrong loving.

Heresy is, then, a way of being anti-historical and anti-social. It is to fail to recognize the space between fiction and fact, to fail to live in the space of the nearly reasonable, the space in which we live—history. Heresy is not apostasy. Apostasy leaves the faith and the family altogether. Heresy remains in the camp, just somehow misguided or misinformed. But apostasy is not nearly the danger that heresy can be. We don't trust apostasy, for it has left. Heresy hasn't left, and we are still listening.

What, exactly, is the danger here? Is it that we shall be washed away, we orthodox? Is it that our faith or social relationships shall be destroyed? Perhaps. There are hazards lying about. In our human creativity, we sometimes step over the line. We grab that fruit and eat. However, we tend to act alone, on our own authority, when we move into heresy. Hence the importance of the social community. And that community is vast, extending around the world and into the democracy of the dead.[2] Heresy has not yet left the family, it is not yet apostasy, but with loving encouragement heresy can perhaps come to see that that small corner of irrationality is only true to the nature of the world. Heresy can then be led back to the happy conflict that is orthodoxy.

Eleanor Stump defends the notion of heresy, but rejects the notion of the heretic.[3] I've been careful to use only the former term. For heresy is a useful term, while heretic is not. The latter names a person, while the former does not. And I'm in no way in favor of naming with annihilation. Orthodoxy should woo heresy, not annihilate one who embraces heresy. To say we ought not burn heretics is a vast understatement. Heresy, no less than orthodoxy, is just trying to be reasonable. Heresy is just trying to figure out the way. But orthodoxy is growing and changing too, and we don't always know where the line is. For as reasonable as we might like to make the world, there is always the bit that is not quite reasonable. And sometimes heresy can point the right way. Heresy should no longer reek of burning human flesh. Rather, it should be discussed in the thick smoke of a peace pipe, around an ancient fire.

---

2. Chesterton uses this phrase.
3. Stump, "Orthodoxy and Heresy."

8

Hope

Suicide is in many cases the result of a loss of hope. In my late wife's last hours, she left a note saying, among other things, that she hadn't lost her faith but that she had lost her hope. Without hope, many perhaps most cannot go on. But what is hope? The example with which I begin may sound as if it is autobiographical. It is not. Rather it is supplied by Gabriel Marcel. It just happens to fit well with my experience.

A young woman is dying. Her lover hopes she will live and not die. And not only does he hope she will live, but he hopes she will live and flourish. What is this hope, this nonsense, this unrealistic picture of the world? We have here, one might suggest, a true denial of the harsh realities of life. The woman is going to die. The young man's desire that she live and flourish is nothing more than wishful thinking, something contrary to reality. We might say the young man is not living in reality, that he is being unrealistic. Hope is unrealistic.

This unrealism is not a radical postmodernism, for this case doesn't behave the way one might expect. The radical postmodern, too, ignores reality, just as does our hopeful young man. But the unrealism of the radical postmodern ignores reality for other reasons, for the radical postmodern doesn't have a reality with which to interact. The radical postmodern, in fact, *can't say* there is no hope, for the radical postmodern lives in an entirely fictional world, ignoring, if not denying, reality. To demand of this young man that he be realistic and that reality is the reason there is no hope, is a curiosity. Isn't it because there is a reality that hope is possible? One reason, then, that radical postmodernism should be rejected is just that it can't make sense of hope, nor even make sense of the reality that hope supposedly ignores. Hope doesn't ignore reality. Radical postmodernism does.

One cannot hope for what one knows has already happened. Hope clearly has a future-oriented nature, much like freedom. Also, much like freedom, the past grounds hope. What past? In hope's case, the past of despair. Here one finds hope's relationship to reality. Gabriel Marcel, in many ways a philosopher of hope, worries that his appeal to despair, betrayal, and suicide will be taken only to sensationalize his philosophy. On the contrary, Marcel tells us despair is always possible and this despair and its betrayals are forced upon us by the world.[1] Yet despair is not alone. Despair, he notes, can be likened to a balance sheet. Suppose all of reality were written down and accounted for on an accountant's balance sheet. When one considers reality, one finds nothing on the sheet whereby credit can be extended. Despair is a state of complete insolvency—the bankruptcy of reality. It is not, so much, that there is nothing real. It is that the real is contingent, weak, and, ultimately, insolvent and powerless. Against this insolvency, this bankruptcy, one finds despair's partner, hope. "Hope," Marcel continues, "consists in asserting that there is at the heart of being, beyond all data, beyond all inventories and all calculations, a mysterious principle which is in connivance with me, which cannot but will that which I will, if what I will deserves to be willed and is, in fact, willed by the whole of my being."[2]

Against this assertion of hope, no use comes of presenting cases and counter-examples. No use comes of saying to the young man that he is unrealistic. No use derives from saying that in so many other cases, young women died. The young man will simply reply, more vehemently, that there is hope! I do not simply *wish*, says the young man, I *assert* that she will live and flourish. Marcel calls this the "prophetic tone of true hope." Marcel tells us something of great importance. "It is of the essence of hope to exclude the consideration of cases; moreover, it can be shown that there exists an ascending dialectic of hope, whereby hope rises to a plane which transcends the level of all possible empirical disproof—the plane of salvation as opposed to that of success in whatever form."[3] Hope

1. Marcel, "Ontological Mystery," 26.
2. Ibid., 28.
3. Ibid., 28.

is no success term. Hope is not empirical. It is not meant to say that one knows all is well here and now. Hope is, instead, a salvific term. The despair we find in living our lives of quiet desperation is not to be denied. Yet despair isn't all there is. Despair is the reality we face when we realize the limits of our freedom—our sin, our finitude, our death. If we place our trust merely in what we can order and reason and rationalize, we ultimately realize the end of our own being. Heresy makes all things smooth. Despair merely recognizes that the smoothness hasn't included all of the real, for not all the real is rational. There is something beyond all calculations, all balance sheets, all accounting. It is hope.

Hope wouldn't be, were there no despair. Only in a world of despair can hope exist. Only in a world of reality misunderstood, or reality mistaken, can hope thrive. If we've got all the answers, if control is within our grasp, then no hope is needed. But when reality experienced doesn't give credit, hope is possible. This is what Marcel calls "the only genuine hope."[4] In contrast, a false hope exists, a hope in ourselves and our own abilities and techniques. We trust progress, we trust that some day we'll be able to figure it out and understand and live in a utopian world. That was *adam*'s thought in the Garden. *adam* thought he'd like to understand good and evil. It seemed worthwhile. But he failed to have the kind of being it would take to understand, without getting entangled in, evil. Hope in our own ability—in our case, our own radical postmodern fictions—isn't true hope. For true hope, there must be recognition of reality.

Marcel suggests that genuine hope is hope that doesn't depend upon us. Hope springs from humility not hubris. Pride doesn't let us see hope, doesn't let us align ourselves with the principles that are beyond us. Pride stands in our way. Pride blinds us to those corners of reality beyond our control. Hope, in contrast, is the ability to see the reality beyond our control and to will with it what is good. One cannot truly hope without admitting that, in fact, the situation is out of one's control. That is why hope is a salvific and not an empirical category. Hope is possible not where we stiffen our wills against the reality we face. It is a relaxation of the will, a recognition of our limits, and a creation of the will. Marcel tells us there is a principle of being in connivance with me that wills what I will. There is a convergence of two things here: my will and the will of the mystery of being. In this convergence, we find the connection between hope and freedom.

4. Ibid., 32.

Fidelity, Marcel says, is ontological. Fidelity trades in being. Fidelity is creative freedom in response to what is. Hope is a recognition that the world is not in my control, but rather that the world must will what I will, when what I will is good and willed with my whole being. Hope raises me up above myself, above my techniques, above my tinkering, above my will, by relaxing me into the good that is, the Real. It saves me from myself and my fictions. True hope is creative fidelity. Fidelity is not adherence to a bunch of rules or principles simply for the sake of the principles. Fidelity is a forward-looking trust in the way the universe is. Creativity is the ever present striving to live well. Hope is the combination of the two, creative fidelity. So at the base of hope is reality, the recognition of our limits, our finitude, our sin, our powerlessness. But hope is reality transformed by creative fidelity. The future will not be like the past. The young woman will not die. She will live and flourish. But for that, we must participate in what we don't understand, what we do not know.

Hope is a very important notion for understanding ourselves and the demand lain upon us by the Real. Hope is what is needed to combat the heresy of radical postmodernism. Yet, radical postmodernism is sure to respond, "all that is well and good, if some reason is forthcoming to think there is a reality, that there is, perhaps, a God. But we have no reason to think there is a reality, much less a God. Therefore, to say we live in history rather than fiction is simply wishful thinking, unfounded hope."

Contrary to this criticism, hope is not wishful thinking, although hope is sometimes contrary to what *appears* to be reality. Radical postmodernism cannot accuse hope of not being realistic, of wishful thinking. Hope is no mere wishful thinking in the teeth of a hard reality. Hope is prophetic. It asserts that the world is neither simply despair nor simply made up of my fantasies. The world is not made of stories I entirely control. Hope asserts, at a level beyond the mechanical, beyond the empirical, beyond the fictional, that the world is not devoid of meaning. Hope makes meaning, for hope is aligned with the forces and principles of the universe that pride cannot recognize. Faith precedes understanding. So does hope. It is very difficult for us, as it has been for humanity down through the ages, to admit that we are not at the center of reality. The Fall teaches that. To admit there might be something other, something I cannot have access to through my own powers, is to admit that I'm not what I think I am, a god.

Obviously what is said here is deeply indebted to Marcel. For that I make no apology. But I must apologize for one thing. Marcel states, at the end of his essay, that creative fidelity need not be construed as rooted directly in the Church or Christianity. He thinks what he says is about the natural, not the supernatural. It is, he says, open to the foundations of any religion. I suspect an error in judgment on his part, a failure to connect history to hope. The use toward which I put hope here is not limited to the natural, nor is it open to just any and all religions. It is meant to be peculiarly historical and therefore peculiarly Christian. A good many people do, in fact, have an experience of creative fidelity in their lives, and many are within a religion other than Christianity and some outside of religion altogether. But if hope is historical, then such creative fidelity finds its true home, I believe, in the historical nature of Christianity, and in the God who created us as historical, if hopeful, beings.

Hope, then, is a reason to choose history over fiction. The possibility of hope forces the Real upon us. But hope is also free and therefore prophetic and not despairing. The radical postmodern *as radical* ultimately cannot have a self and as such, hope is not possible. But hope is an assertion and the radical postmodern *as human* can assert that there is a reality, thereby stepping into humility, and thereby into hope. One can hope the world is not so bleak as to be nothing more than imagined by us. I propose, therefore, a reason to reject radical postmodernism's error. It is our freedom to hope, which even the radical postmodern has, but only derivatively so. The truly radical postmodern person is a fiction, and a fiction has no freedom. The radical postmodern person *can* hope against the despair and loneliness of the radically postmodern world. The radical postmodern person can hope there is something salvific about the world, and hence have a starting place in creative fidelity. But the radical postmodern *as radical* can do so only by stealing freedom from nowhere.

9

Death

When my older son was about nine, he sat crying at his school desk, where he daily did his home school work. Between sobs, he told me about a bug he wanted to keep as a pet. That's fine, said I, but why the tears? Cries unabated then rolled from his little body. No words could squeeze past the tears. As time went by, I asked him again, why the tears? Ian spoke his sorrow, punctuated by sobs: "I was working at my math questions. A bug crawled onto my book. I watched him crawl. He crawled up my hand. He walked back down to my book. I played with him, putting my finger in front of him. The bug walked around my finger. I used the end of my pencil. He went around it a few times and then went to the edge of my book. He began to walk the very edge. I put my pencil's side against the edge of my book for the bug to walk around. We played this game for a while, when I thought he'd gone to the front of my pencil." Now the wails of sorrow rolled again, my son's body shaking in grief and shock. I supplied the end of the story, surmising that the bug had gone to the back and was crushed as my son rolled his pencil over him. My son wailed his pain, his sorrow, his grief.

Why is death so important? Why is *this* death so important? Many a bug had fallen prey to my son before. Although not a wanton kind of killer, although not a boy who pulls the wings off flies to watch them squirm, my son, nonetheless, had killed a good number of insects. This death was different. This death was the death of a friend.

The death of a stranger typically doesn't affect us. Perhaps it should. Although we show respect when the hearse and procession go by, we don't typically feel grief. A grieving death is a named death. We must first have named the dead when the person was alive, and we must name the death itself. Without both namings, we have no share in the pain. My son named the dead in life. The two played. My son named the death. Indeed, he did the dying himself, for he was the instrument of his friend's death. My son was implicated in this death, dragged down to death, entombed in death. All death became his. Death is named by us, only at the cost of carving our own tombstone.

Sin roots death. Just as sin is universal, so is death. Sin first makes us want to hide from God. Adam and Eve not only hide in the Garden but clothe themselves to shield their shame. God forewarns them that death follows from eating the tree of the knowledge of good and evil. There beside the tree of the knowledge of good and evil is the tree of life. Why choose the only forbidden tree? Why not the other one, the tree of promise, health, eternal life? Is death attractive? Does Adam not understand?

Death is not alone among the destroyers, but it is the final one. Death is not something toward which we look with pleasure and desire. Although death can bring us an end of suffering, and so death can be a kind of healing, death itself is not preferable to a good life. We know, somehow, that life is valuable and worthwhile, yet we are vague about why, exactly, it is. We live in history, and history is full of horror. We wish to run from history, toward objectivity on the one hand, or fiction on the other. As we run toward objectivity, we run from meaning. As we run toward fiction, we run from reality. How ironic that death is a kind of unreality. In death we lack being. We know that we exist barely above nothing. We know that we are conscious and aware, but we don't know how consciousness works or exactly why we have it. We know that but for some power, we slip into unconsciousness permanently. Consciousness is strange. One minute a person is alive, thinking, and talking. The next, she slips away. When consciousness goes, the person goes, leaving only a body. When consciousness goes, nothing is truly left. We know that we exist barely above nothing. The greatest danger we fear, the greatest danger we face, is slipping into nothingness—death, the abyss of unreality.

What is so odd is the peculiar disappearance of death. These days, many suggest there is nothing to fear in death, for death is no more than the cessation of consciousness. Well, true enough, if there is nothing to us but mortal being, if there is nothing to us but the mere material working of the brain and its physiology. These days there is nothing to fear in death, for there will be no one there to do the fearing. Death disappears, for we are never truly alive. And yet we wonder. We wonder if that is all there is. However, even if we do not fear death, perhaps we should desire long, long lives, for consciousness itself seems worthwhile.

In "The Myth of Sisyphus," Albert Camus claims that the only real philosophical question is the question of suicide. He then proceeds in an ingenious way to defend the claim that suicide is wrong. But why? After telling us there is no God, and explaining that all we have is our experiences, one after another, Camus tells us suicide is wrong because it brings the series of our experiences to a shorter end than it otherwise would have. Is just being conscious for a longer period of time worthwhile? Is this why we care about death? Surely not. What is morally wrong with shortening the list of experiences one has? Perhaps the issue isn't one of morality but simply that it is a good thing to be conscious. Yet although Camus assumes the opposite, not all consciousness is worthwhile. Staying alive and conscious just to have other experiences, when all those experiences are negative, nasty, brutish, and long, seems wrongheaded. No, death's sting lies elsewhere.

Most, if not all, of us desire life to be good. For many of us, life is not good. There is a danger in confusing one's own experience with everyone else's. A danger exists also of generalizing from one's own experience to common human experience. Neither are good moves logically. Yet the desire to live a good life seems universal enough. Whatever the good life is, I want it. Should I have it, I don't want it to end. I don't want to die.

We are not unlike the ancient Greeks and Romans. The Epicureans thought death ought not to be feared, for the world is material and death is just the end of the material order of one's body. Death was thought a thing of fiction with no basis in reality. There not being any life after death, death contained no fear. In fact, it is the fear of death that leads to so much havoc in one's life that the truly good life cannot be obtained. For the Epicureans, the fear of death is irrational and based on a false conception of the universe. If one wanted to be happy, one should overcome the false fear. Likewise, the Stoics believed death was not to be feared for, like all things in life, death should be faced with peace and tranquility. The world is ordered by Reason and there is nothing to be done. Reason will march right over us anyway. In our deterministic, materialistic world, life is no more than one event after another and there is, indeed, nothing to be done. Death is just another event, not to be feared, not to be of concern.

Yet the fear of death is not so easily dismissed, whether by ancient philosophy or modern materialism. We spend billions of dollars trying to stay alive as long as possible and in as good health as possible. We have a philosophy that says nothing really counts and yet we count death as something to be avoided. Postmodernism, too, has problems with death, for death brings the fiction to an end. In fact, death should be the ultimate fiction, yet we know we can not write death out of the story. Death cannot be avoided.

Death is a problem, no matter how we talk about it. We don't want to die, unless our life is taken by us not to be worthwhile because of extraordinary pain and suffering. Those who believe our lives have no point or meaning may also see life as painful, once that belief becomes one's driving force. Camus suggests that a human is most alive, most conscious when, like Sisyphus, she turns to embrace the absurdity of our existence, when she turns to walk down the hill once more to engage in her absurd rolling of the rock to the top of the hill. Camus has, I think, difficulty getting a moral claim against suicide off the ground, given his views of absurdity. For surely the absurdity of life makes neither living nor dying more valuable than the other. Why not kill ourselves; what value is there in consciousness? Camus was not, perhaps, miserable, as some might think his writings suggest. Yet Camus, like many others, fooled himself into believing life is worth living, all the while saying that nothing more than a random or deterministic order exists in the universe. Pronouncing the problem of death resolved by saying that one simply wants more conscious experiences is itself absurd. At best only a fleeting, self-deceptive happiness is possible there. Rather like the ancient Epicureans and Stoics, many contemporary determinists, materialists, existentialists, and radical postmodernists simply pronounce death stingless. Such pronouncements should strike us, I believe, as crazy. I do not want to die, if death is simply the end of consciousness—I like consciousness. Yet consciousness alone is not enough. Camus's experience for experience's own sake appears wrongheaded. I don't want consciousness *per se*. If pain, suffering, and torture are all I feel, why want to be conscious? No, I am more than experience. I am an "I." It is *I* who wants to live and it is *I* who wants the whole thing to mean something. I want to live because living is a good thing. I am not just a series of events and experiences.

The Epicureans and Stoics seemed to have an answer, but as St. Athanasius pointed out, the philosophers had so few true followers. So it is today. How many true radical postmodernists are there, how many true determinists, how many true materialists? So we might ask, can our contemporary solution to death succeed any better than the ancient ones? The Epicureans simply avoid the issue by counseling that death doesn't really exist, there being nothing about matter to die. They ignore death by defining it out of existence. There is nothing to fear, for death is the end of the fearing consciousness. For the Stoics, if death is ignored as something that must come, there is nothing to fear. Ignorance leads to freedom from fear. For us, the shoe fits otherwise. While we pretend not to fear death, and so ignore it, in actuality we so fear death that we ignore it. That is our solution. Death dies by denial; death dies a death of intentional shunning. But death will not, cannot, be ignored. It conquers in the end. As Pascal says: "It is easier to put up with death without thinking about it, than with the idea of death when there is no danger of it."[1] Death is the real end of our lives. When a person slips into the final unconsciousness, the person is gone.

If death is not to be feared, at least it ought to be avoided. Yet how can we do that? Death slips us into history in fixed and permanent terms. We cannot change our histories once dead. Death is the end of history; it is the final corruption of being. St. Athanasius had it right. In the creation of the world by the Word, being is called into existence. We and all created matter exist just above nothing. Yet we humans are different. He writes:

> Grudging existence to none, therefore, [God] made all things out of nothing through His own Word, our Lord Jesus Christ; and of all these His earthly creatures He reserved especial mercy for the race of men. Upon them, therefore, upon men who, as animals, were essentially impermanent, He bestowed a grace which other creatures lacked—namely, the impress of His own Image, a share in the reasonable being of the very Word Himself, so that, reflecting Him and themselves becoming reasonable and

---

1. Pascal, *Pensees*, 49.

expressing the Mind of God even as He does, though in limited degree, they might continue for ever in the blessed and only true life of the saints in paradise.[2]

Athanasius continues on to tell us that we humans fall under the "natural law of death" when we sin. That is, death is our natural state. We shall not just die, says he, but we shall remain in a state of death. According to Athanasius, death is natural. Death naturally pulls us into the abyss of nonbeing. Yet although our natural tendency is toward death, we are also made with Reason, the impress of God. Once we sin, what is natural became normal. Our tendency toward corruption ceases to be countermanded by the impress of God and death takes over.

We are called out of nothing into being. Our being, therefore, is contingent. Our being doesn't have to be. Athanasius says: "the presence of the Word with . . . [humans] . . . shielded them even from natural corruption."[3] In the Fall, corruption ran riot among humanity, even to a point more than natural. So we are left fallen into corruption, for we tarnish the image of God in us. Reason itself is left to rot. The gift we are given is destroyed by sin. So although we are by nature impermanent, the Word in creation gives us the gift of eternal life. In our sin, we return to our natural state of death, slouching toward nonexistence. Death is our enemy; corruption is our enemy. Our enemy is our fragile human finite nature. We cannot get ourselves out of this hole. We cannot save ourselves and overcome death. It is the final limit, the last boundary, the fixity of all fixities. No one escapes death.

Yet, says Athanasius, death is not to be feared but derided and despised. "All the disciples of Christ despise death; they take the offensive against it and, instead of fearing it by the sign of the cross and by faith in Christ trample on it as on something dead."[4] Before Christ came and did his work, even the holiest of men feared death, says Athanasius. Now the Christians do not. Fear was replaced by despising. This is, says Athanasius, a reason to take Christianity as true. Death is dead, death is

---

2. Athanasius, *On the Incarnation*, 28. It is worth noting that although humans are given this special mercy, it costs them dearly, for they become with this reason, also responsible in the way the natural order does not. This need not make us more valuable than the rest of nature, only different. In the end, God redeems the whole universe, not just humans.

3. Ibid., 30.

4. Ibid., 57.

overcome. How? By Jesus' incarnation. In His incarnation, Jesus took on human form and yet lived His life by the power of God. The very Word that created the world in the first place, that gave humanity the ability to live forever, came to be among us, to live the life that we should have lived. In Jesus' doing so, and then by dying and rising from the dead, death is overcome. Jesus lived and died in history so that our history could be transformed.

Athanasius tells us this.

> Even so, if anyone still doubts the conquest of death, after so many proofs and so many martyrdoms in Christ and such daily scorn of death by His truest servants, he certainly does well to marvel at so great a thing, but he must not be obstinate in unbelief and disregard of plain facts. No, he must be like the man who wants to prove the property of asbestos, and like him who enters the conqueror's dominions to see the tyrant bound. He must embrace the faith of Christ, this disbeliever in the conquest of death and come to His teaching. Then he will see how impotent death is and how completely conquered. Indeed, there have been many former believers and deriders who, after they became believers, so scorned death as even themselves to become martyrs for Christ's sake.[5]

Athanasius presents a dual-pronged apologetic. First, there is the appeal to martyrdom as proof of Christ's overcoming death. In martyrdom, we see the derision of death by the true believer. Death is despised, not feared. Martyrdom embraces all that is good about life, when life is found in God. The second is the appeal to faith. If you can't accept another's death as proof, try Christianity as you might try asbestos. Walk in the coals of death, and see if they only warm, rather than burn, your feet. But not without the teaching of the Lord himself.

Death is not to be feared not because it is ignored, but rather because it is embraced. Yet not death of any kind. Chesterton points out that the Church has always been against suicide but enthusiastic about martyrdom. This is not inconsistent, he says.[6] Martyrdom calls for commitment to something outside oneself, suicide a commitment only to oneself. Suicide is wrong, then, not as Camus has it—because it reduces

---

5. Ibid., 58, 59.
6. Chesterton, *Orthodoxy*, 73.

the number of experiences one might have—but rather because it takes oneself to be the judge of what's valuable. Suicide is a kind of idolatry.

Death is to be embraced. It is not to be feared but lived through with the courage of a life transformed by the maker of the world, the Word. The being of God keeps us afloat ontologically and it is that same being who rebuilds us after we fall and the impress of God is marred.

I began with my older son's exposure to death as a shared experience. I'll end there too. After my father died, my family went to my mother's to visit. Ian was about four years old. We drove past the cemetery where my father was buried. My little boy looked out the car window as we rolled past the graves. He paused, turned, and looked at me. He said, "Dad, gravestones are like bookmarks."

I wept.

10

Miracle

I HAVE PRAYED FOR MIRACLES. Hasn't everyone? When the worst of life drags us into dark corners, don't we all ask for a change in the rules, or at least a change of venue? While I'm sure I've prayed for miracles, I'm less sure I've seen very many, at least one of the type of which David Hume is critical, although I'm inclined to believe I have seen a few. Among many other things, my late wife was prone to extreme vaginal bleeding that sometimes required us to take her to the emergency room. On one occasion when we were just about to drive her to the hospital, we asked little six-year old Ian if he would touch Mom's tummy and pray that God would make her better. He did, and God did. The bleeding stopped immediately and we avoided yet another hospital trip. It is notable that the Scriptures talk of the need for child-like faith. Perhaps my own general skepticism keeps my prayers from being answered.

A miracle is thought to be a breaking of the laws of nature, but that is no great feat for the One who made the laws. And if Chesterton is right, God made no "laws" at all. A law of nature is typically understood as fixed and unchanging. A law of nature is the way it is because of some universal deterministic web. Yet we have seen from Chesterton and the "ethics of elfland,"[1] that the so-called laws of nature are not fixed. Alternatively, God makes the daisies new each day, one by one. What, then, is a miracle? What counts as an example of one? If we are to start with an example, we might as well begin with the grandest one of all. Some may be tempted to

---

1. See above, chapter 2, n. 5.

suggest the resurrection as the grandest, but another is more fundamental than that. Let us start with the Incarnation. The biblical story can not be told without its central character, Jesus the Word Incarnate. If we can at least partially understand this grandest of miracles, then we will have gone some way toward an account of miracle in general.

David Hume says, in his ingenious argument against miracles, that a miracle has two aspects. First, it must break a law of nature. Second, it must be divinely authored. The first suggestion typically gets the focus, for there isn't much splashier than the breaking of a law of nature. So we think. But as the rules of fairyland suggest, the laws of nature aren't really laws, and therefore can't be broken. There's nothing permanently fixed about the "laws" in the first place. In other words, the laws are contingent to begin with. Indeed, philosophers also say that the regularities of nature are only statistical regularities. There is no force of logic or true necessity in them. So, there is nothing to break. One might think, instead, of the possibility that they can be wrinkled.

And perhaps not even that. The second prong of Hume's fork is the claim to divinity. How is one to know that some event or other is divinely authored? Here we have the straw that broke the theological camel's back. How can it be, asks the theologian of modernity, that the accidental truths of history ever teach us of the necessities of metaphysics? How can we derive universal truths about all that is—God, freewill, morality—from the merely contingent things of history? This is the very heart of the matter, the core of this book's entire argument. The accidental truths of history are the very place in which live the necessities of metaphysics.

God does not make a world distant from the divine. God makes a world through the Incarnate Son, the Word. In the beginning, God creates the world by speaking it. With the divine Word, the world is made. Not much is closer to one's being that one's word. One's word is the natural extension of oneself; it is one's character made public, made social, made accessible.[2] Hence, the loathsomeness of lying. To lie is to fail in one's being. To speak the truth is to present reality. One's words, when true, express the world. One's words, when a lie, are empty, expressing unreality and our tendency toward nothingness. Yet words detach, and so when one's words are separated from oneself, they can take on something of a life of their own. Thus, one's words must be spoken with care.

---

2. See Berry, "Standing by Words," for some valuable insights.

If we are to be persons of integrity, we can not fail to take responsibility for the words we utter.

Certainly God cannot fail to do so. When God speaks the world, the divine Word is imprinted in the world. This is the key to miracle. As Athanasius reports,

> ... suppose they confess that there is a Word of God, that He is the Governor of all things, that in Him the Father wrought the creation, that by His providence the whole receives light and life and being, and that He is King over all, so that He is known by means of the works of His providence and through Him the Father. Suppose they confess all this, what then? Are they unknowingly turning the ridicule against themselves? The Greek philosophers say that the universe is a great body, and they say truly, for we perceive the universe and its parts with our sense. But if the Word of God is in the universe, which is a body, and has entered into it in its every part, what is there surprising or unfitting in our saying that He has entered also in the human nature? If it were unfitting for Him to have embodied Himself at all, then it would be unfitting for Him to have entered into the universe, and to be giving light and movement by His providence to all things in it, because the universe, as we have seen, is itself a body. But if it is right and fitting for Him to enter into the universe and to reveal Himself through it, then, because humanity is part of the universe along with the rest, it is no less fitting for Him to appear in a human body, and to enlighten and to work through that.[3]

Here is Athanasius' understanding of the Incarnation, the Word spoken into the world.

> The Word is embodied already in the world spoken by the Word Himself. To become Incarnate in human form is merely an extension of the Word's imprint on the world. Yet the being of the world, left in its purely natural state, its finite state, will tend toward dissolution. Contingent being is corruptible, all of it. We humans were special, though, for unlike all other created things, humans were initially made in God's image and we were therefore eternally alive. When we tarnished that image as we sinned, our being tended again toward corruption. In the Incarnation, the Word showed through His power and glory, that even corruptible human being could become incorruptible. In being made initially in the image of God, we had an opportunity that would

---

3. Athanasius, *On the Incarnation*, 76.

not pass to us again, once we sinned. Unless, that is, the Word became Incarnate in human flesh, living like us, living among us, showing us the transformative power of God. We are lifted out of the muck of destruction and corruption and onto the plain of the divine. This is the truest of all miracles, mere contingent flesh transfigured into eternal reality.[4]

What, then, is a miracle? A miracle is the presence of the Word among us. When Christ heals the ill, changes the water into wine, or makes the blind to see, he does nothing that is not, for him, normal. So miracles are not breaks in the laws of nature, for there would be no nature except for the saving, gracious presence of the Word. Nature merely continues to operate under the power of the Word. Of course, that miracles are divine is the basis for all being, for all being is divinely held together.

But we, and the entire world, are fallen, caught up in the vileness of evil and sin. The final miracle is the calling together of being for the final transformation into a new heaven and earth. This transfiguration to come is the extension of God's Word, actively participating in the world. While not complete, the Kingdom of God is present here now, and the process begun. Miracle was released into history when God first spoke the Word and made the world.

But what role does miracle play, if all events are miraculous? Why does Jesus turn water to wine, why raise Lazarus from the dead? Some miracles are, admittedly, more splashy than others. I would be impressed should someone be raised from the dead before my eyes. Sometimes we think some special thing happens when a person sees a miracle, that is, one of the splashy kind. Miracles, then, are understood as a kind of argument for God's existence, or as showing that Jesus was divine. But this is not the best understanding of the role of miracle, for it relies on a faulty understanding of the role of argument.

4. Ibid.

11

Reason

One of my graduate school professors in philosophy asked me where I thought I stood compared to other graduate students in our department. His particular question was about my intelligence. When I replied "in the middle: I'm not as smart as X and smarter than Y," my professor thought I'd gotten it right. In some senses, being a "professional" philosopher can be extraordinarily hard on one's self-esteem. We are trained, in fact, although perhaps not in so many words, to size up the other person's argument (or intelligence!) and try to punch holes in it. We are trained to size up just how smart the other person is by trying to show that that person's reasoning is faulty. Of course, there are no courses in "sizing up the intelligence of your interlocutor" but nevertheless, one does size them up on a regular basis. This puts reason in, I think, an unreasonable role. It also is bad for one's soul.

Pascal asked the following penetrating question. "Why is it that the lame person does not annoy us when a lame mind does? It is because a lame person realizes that we walk straight, but a lame mind declares that it is we who are limping."[1] Pascal rightly calls attention to what we think we have at stake in our reason. No challenge to our reason can go unchecked, for after all, it is *me* that is challenged when my reasoning is.

Reason is easily thought of as right thinking, and right thinking is, of course, what *I* do. If I believe the wall is white, then I believe "the wall is white" is a true statement. To believe is to be committed to the

---

1. Pascal, *Pensees*, 32.

truth of what one believes. To reason to a belief is to understand one's reason as pointing to the reasonableness of the belief and hence the truth of the belief. We thus treat *our* reasoning as something special, as privileged, as giving us the truth. So the beliefs I end up with, supposing I got those beliefs reasonably, are taken by me to be true. The minds of others, when disagreeing with mine, are lame. To lame minds, I take offense. What could be more natural, since, of course, my beliefs are true! The lame mind challenges me. Since I am right, the lame mind is wrong, and since the mind is lame, I am doubly insulted. It would be odd indeed to say I believe the wall is white and yet believe also that "the wall is white" is false.

What real connection is there amongst reason, belief, and truth? Surely not all my beliefs are true. Yet I would be taken as odd should I say that I believe some statement and yet take that very statement as false. My beliefs are *mine*—I like them, cherish them, and sometime might even die for them. Yet I know they are likely not all true. Whence reason, then? Reason gives me true beliefs. In reason I trust, and yet what is reason that I should so trust?

Reasons are arguments. An argument is a string of propositions, a special string of propositions. If I take the propositions in an argument to be true save the final one, I should take the final one to be true as well. Robert Nozick points out some important things about argument. When we mention that philosophers argue, the child often thinks that we yell at one another. The metaphors we use in referring to argument shed light upon this child-like observation. We philosophers are prone to say, "That's a knock down, drag out argument." Or "that argument is very powerful." Or perhaps we say that the argument was strong or overwhelming. Nozick suggests that perhaps what we need is an argument so strong that if the recipient doesn't believe its conclusion, powerful reverberations are set up in the brain so the recipient dies.[2] The implications of Nozick's not-so-subtle observation are protean.

How does the will play in here? Even if an argument threatens one's life, one can still resist its conclusions, sort of like when a thief threatens one with a gun and says "your money or your life." One can still refuse to give over one's money. Refusing the thief's request might be foolish, but the will is a powerful thing. Yet the will is not the only thing that can influence one's reason. Pascal writes: "If you put the world's great-

---

2. Nozick, *Philosophical Explanations*, 4, 5.

est philosopher on a plank wider than he needs, but with a precipice beneath, however strongly his reason may convince him of his safety, his imagination will prevail. Many would be unable to contemplate the idea without going pale and sweating."[3] Fear can overrule one's reason. Similarly, so can love and passions of all types. Reason cannot, in fact, be thought of in fullness without recourse to the emotions. Reason always comes attached.

No embarrassment should attend this discovery. Philosophers from Plato and Aristotle on down through history tried to shed reason of its emotional cousins. Yet the cousins can't be divorced from the family. Plato, for as much as he wants to ban poetry from the republic, himself is such a poetic writer that one can be moved to laughter and tears by his descriptions. Aristotle, whose Unmoved Mover is nothing but pure thought, can't deny that the dramatic arts involve the catharsis of the passions. One's emotions put one in touch with aspects of reality that pure reason can not. One is not easily motivated by pure argument alone to help the needy. Better to have felt their pain. Moral development occurs in the context of both intellectual and emotional response.

So will and emotion attend reason, and reason therefore is not the only source of knowledge. Reason has limits. Pascal locates these limits in our state. We are both glorious and wretched. "A human being is only a reed, the weakest in nature, but he is a thinking reed. To crush him, the whole universe does not have to arm itself. A mist, a drop of water, is enough to kill him. But if the universe were to crush the reed, the man would be nobler than his killer, since he knows that he is dying, and that the universe has the advantage over him."[4] We are stretched out between the infinite and nothing, always grasping after truth, but never finding certainty. Reason can only give us so much.

The lame mind returns again to assault us. This time, however, the lame mind is our own. We must, in confronting the lame mind, understand the limits of our own reason. "Man's greatness lies in his capacity to recognize his wretchedness."[5] So reason requires of us humility. Pascal writes: "It is unfair that anyone should be devoted to me, although it can happen with pleasure, and freely. I should mislead those in whom I quickened this feeling, because I am no one's ultimate end, and cannot

3. Pascal, *Pensees*, 17.
4. Ibid., 72, 73.
5. Ibid., 36.

satisfy them. Am I not near death? So the object of their attachment will die. Therefore just as I should be guilty if I caused a falsehood to be believed, however gently persuasive I had been and however pleasurably it had been believed, giving me pleasure too, in the same way I am guilty if I make myself loved and if I attract people to become devoted to me."[6]

My importance as human being has limits. I slouch toward nonbeing. Encouraging devotion to me is encouraging a misplacement of affection. Pascal relates the encouragement of devotion to oneself to the guilt of arguing falsehood. No matter how gently I persuade, and no matter how happy false belief makes my interlocutor, falseness is destructive. So is the encouragement.

The lame mind reminds me, by mirror reflection, of myself. I'm accused of my fallibility, and recognize by the very emotional response I have to its accusations, that I have a humble estate. Whether I also have a humble response is up to me. Humility cannot be separated from reason. Whether reason responds to its humble estate affects my judgment about my reason. Reason thus brings us to the edge of emotion and emotion brings us face to face with the limits of reason. Reason opens us to possibilities other than itself. It leads us to the foot of truth, but it cannot scale the mountain for us.

---

6. Ibid., 7.

12

Faith

FAITH IS REASON UNMASKED. The lame mind is a kind of magic mirror which tells only the truth. We are not the most fair in the land. When the lame mind accuses us, it reflects back our natures as limited reasoners, less than perfect. We are pushed into the realm of the passions and the will, where humility presents us with our true selves. Reason cannot take us all the way, on its own, to truth. When the lame mind accuses us of being lame-minded, it accuses us of thinking crookedly. We are offended, hardly able to recognize our own reaction. We react vehemently against our accuser, naming the lame mind substandard, or stupid, or silly. Of course, sometimes the lame mind is lame, and the problem isn't with us. Sometimes our response to the lame mind is accurate. But even if we are right about thinking correctly, and the lame mind is truly lame, our reaction is, as Pascal points out, annoyance rather than sympathy. We are typically sure that we think aright, criticism notwithstanding. The negative attitude with which we react is so common one wonders if there isn't a lesson to be learned somewhere in our very emotional responses to the lame mind's accusations.

Humility presents us with our true selves. "Humility" is a complex word, rooted in the ancient word from which we also draw "humus." Humility deals with the humus, the dirt on which we tread.[1] But dirt is fantastic stuff. Sure, we walk on it, but it also grows the grass and plants of all sorts. It is the stuff from which springs life itself. Humus is humble,

---

1. See Bloom, *Beginning to Pray*, 35.

of lowly estate. It reminds us of our true state in the universe: lowly and yet somehow the source of life.

Humility has both ontological and attitudinal aspects. The ontological is reflected in sentences like this: "He comes from a humble background." Such judgments imply that humility is necessarily lowly, as if there is a scale of value in the universe, and someone who is humble exists on the low end. But this suggestion falls short of the truth, for if there is a scale in the universe, it probably doesn't reflect our "accidental" circumstances such as being born in poverty or as a person of little means.

Nevertheless, we say things like this: "Although she is of humble background, she is a very proud person." Pride, of course, can be the opposite of humility but it isn't always. When we say a person is proud and yet humble, we typically don't mean to say her pride is contrary to her humility. Indeed, pride is something like good self-esteem. To say she has pride, in such contexts, is to say she knows who she is. She knows her value doesn't derive from her standing in society or her lack of wealth or status. Rather, she is valuable because she is who she is, and her pride in herself reflects that. This sense of pride is captured in the following: "Have some pride in yourself" or "Where's your pride?"

Oddly enough, this sense of pride runs roughly parallel to one sense of the term "humility." Those who are humble have a proper view of themselves, thinking no less highly and no more lowly of themselves than is appropriate. Pride and humility in these contexts are two sides of the same coin. To have pride is to be appropriately humble. One should believe in oneself (have pride) and that requires accurately viewing oneself (humility). None of this captures the contrast found in "although she is from a humble background, she is a very proud person." Here the contrast is between her humble state (her status in society—poverty, or at least little means, etc.) and her accurate understanding of her value (which does not derive from her status in society, but from her status as a human, or her own character). To be "of humble estate," then, does not reflect an ontological status but a social one. Nevertheless, to be of humble estate refers to a state, rather than an attitude, and as such points us in the right direction.

Humility as a state of being relies upon a fixed scale of value in the universe, something no mere social status reflects. What is the worth of a human being? The answer depends upon answering a further question, viz., "compared to what?" One's accurate self-judgment that one is an excellent basketball player is dependent upon comparing oneself to other basketball players. If, indeed, one perceives one's ability as a ball player accurately, the judgment can be a humble one. It is one that gets one's position in the basketball universe rightly captured and characterized. But one's accurate self-judgment that one is an excellent human being is a tougher thing. One must measure oneself against humans, against the standard of humanity. So here we verge on the edge of ontological territory. What does it mean to be human? Is there some scale against which to judge oneself? Can one judge oneself as a human without reference to other values in the universe? If humans are made in God's image, mustn't God be in focus as well? When humans compare themselves to God, perhaps we truly are of "humble estate." God is infinite, we are finite, and the gap is much bigger than any of us can imagine. So one's judgment about humility—one's judgment about one's true worth—has ontological overtones.

Humility, too, has an attitudinal aspect. This deals, of course, with one's will. In ancient times, when one entered the chamber of royalty, one humbled oneself. This seems foreign to us now, with our democratic equality. Yet we know the concept. We humble ourselves before the wealthy when we want something of them. We humble ourselves before police officers when we've been caught speeding, hoping we'll be let off. But such humility smacks of groveling. People who grovel lack self-respect. They have no pride. We believe, these days, that all people are created equal. Groveling knows no legitimacy.

Morally, no one need grovel or humble herself before another *human*. But what if this is the wrong comparison, rooted as it is in Enlightenment, modernist principles? What if we compare ourselves not to other finite beings, but to the reality beyond our reason? What if we humble ourselves in the face of the discovery that our reason can't stand alone, that it doesn't give us truth with guarantees? Reality appears one step beyond our intellectual reach. In the face of this discovery, one can decide to view oneself more accurately and understand that passions and the will play vital roles in our commitments and beliefs. Under these conditions, there are two ways to respond. One is simply to assume that the lame mind is wrong, and go on in arrogance to suppose that nothing is awry with one's own reasoning. The other is to open the door to faith.

Faith is reason unmasked. Reason, left alone in its nakedness, cannot stand, and must be surrounded by the other aspects of our humanity, our passions and our will. The will can enable us to take the attitude of humility before the limitations we face, and wonder. We can wonder, "what if there is a transcendent reality?" We can wonder, "what if we can't get along without our human community?" We can wonder, "what if there is a God?"

Karl Jaspers draws a clear distinction between philosophical faith and religious faith.[2] Philosophical faith continues on its quest, constantly on the move, open to possibilities. It's unwilling to take any particular myth and root it into history, making a universal for all. Religious faith, in contrast, does just that. Religious faith, says Jaspers, takes some myth or story or historical accident and universalizes it for all humanity. Is Jaspers right here? Does he rightly suggest that authentic humanity must always be open to the myths being false? Are we forced into an existentialist quagmire of openness, the kind of openness to our historicity that points only to our contingency, only to our ultimate inability to "get it right," only to our finitude?

As a philosopher, I see why Jaspers believes this. Beginning with us and our categories, where else could one end up? Isn't the move to religion the worst kind of faith? It leaves everything closed and answered, when we know that reason won't take us further than the questions. Am I not better off recognizing my limitations and throwing off the authority of religion? Under these conditions, I can at least live authentically in my finitude. But why are questions better than answers? Hasn't Jaspers run into the questions about the questions? Why isn't Jasper's authentic human person stuck in an infinite loop, asking again and again, "Why stop here?" Hasn't he once again reasserted reason as the stopping place? Here reason is understood as limit. As limit, it cannot take us to truth, even the truth of questioning.

Jaspers, of course, calls this faith "philosophical faith." So faith is, indeed, reason unmasked. But why place one's faith in the questions rather than in some myth or other? Jaspers, as the other existentialists, are still moderns. They haven't taken the step to the postmodern, let alone the radical postmodern. The radical postmodern will take any myth and live in that myth until boredom sets in. But here we must return to history, the space between the modern and the postmodern, between the objectivity of the real world and the world of fiction. It is in history that answers are found. Faith cannot be separated from our historicity, nor

2. Jaspers, *Philosophy of Existence*.

can our historicity be separated from our finitude. Our finitude slouches toward the abyss of meaninglessness. Yet history cannot be understood without reference to what lies beyond. We are inclined, as Jaspers suggests, to think of religious faith as slouching toward meaninglessness. When we fixate on a single version of how the universe is, we make a leap toward history as itself being fixed. History lived is not fixed, and neither is the religious life of one committed to God. One's religious life is lived out in a dynamic unity between the transcendence of reality and the stories we tell ourselves, in the space of history. Jaspers thus mischaracterizes religion, for he leaves little room for mystery. Mystery is the core of religious faith.

We treat faith (and here I move beyond philosophical faith) as if it were something one wills. "I choose to be a believer," I pronounce. While the will certainly plays a role in faith, faith is also a gift, something over which one does not have complete control. One cannot choose to believe that one has no name or no Social Security number. One cannot choose not to have faith, if one has it, at least not easily. One can choose not to act on one's faith, but that is a different matter. Faith is a given. And so is unfaith. But just as one can choose not to act on one's faith, one can choose not to act on one's unfaith. Thus faith is related to hope, for one can choose a hopeful stance. Hope moves us toward the historical. In our lives lived in history, the future isn't fixed. Hope and faith go hand in hand, in humility, toward something that is beyond us, something we cannot control. But hope and faith, and especially faith, has a sacramental aspect. Sacraments we cannot control. We cannot just think them into being. So faith, beyond being reason unmasked, is a sacrament, an outward sign of an inward grace. Faith is a grasping of God in the very physical nature of the world. Sacrament comes to the fore.

13

Sacrament

When my wife Susan and I were dating, and we first visited my hometown, we stopped at a small store for, as I remember, some film. Susan and I got out of the car and gave each other a big bear hug, right there in the parking lot. Now in San Francisco that wouldn't be a big thing. But in small-town Canada, such hugs (except among the young) are still considered, well, "inappropriate." Nevertheless, a large man—tall and hefty, like I am—smiled and asked if we were sharing the love. I said sure, and gave him a big hug too! He threw his head back in a great roar of laughter, then looked at me with his eyes twinkling and said, "You know, I like you! Thanks!" I'm not entirely sure why I hugged a total stranger. I know, however, it was a moment of overflowing love. It was, in short, sacramental. Sacramentalism takes us beyond reason.

Reason can never be thought of as pure. Because it is emotionally tinged—we withdraw in fear, we are attracted by laughter—reason cannot stand alone. The will can resist reason, or give in to its apparent inevitability. These emotional and volitional contingencies are situational—historical, if you will. Reason thus always points beyond itself, falling short of capturing the Real. History is the space in which we live our lives, and whatever the reality that gives us boundaries, we are contributors to it. Yet we have no final control. History is bound by a Reality beyond our decisions. We are left responding with the hope for meaningfulness, contributing what we can to the edges of the Real.

Jaspers, Camus, and others admit we come to the edge of reason. We must leap into authenticity. But whence this leap, should there be nothing Real? The leap betrays its hopefulness and its faith. Otherwise it is despair, an arbitrary longing for a better place for our finite being in the universe. But history isn't fiction. While we are stuck with our beliefs, we are wooed by hope. Why not choose hope and openness to God over mere philosophical faith with never ending questions, simply for the sake of the questions? If the Real is merely transcendent, then we truly are to be pitied, for the transcendent exists beyond our reason. But Christianity has no merely transcendent God. If it did, we would be no better off than those with philosophical faith. Christianity is different, for at its center is a God immanent in the world.

Let me put to rest a claim often made by Christians, namely, that Christianity is unique in its doctrine of the Incarnation. It is not. Other religions, Hinduism in particular, have incarnated gods. What is unique about the Christian understanding of the Incarnation is its central salvific role, indeed, its central creative role, in Christian teaching. We must begin with this central doctrine, indeed this central miracle, of the Christian faith, the Incarnation. As noted in "Miracle," the resurrection of a human from the grave is often pointed to as the central miracle of Christianity. St. Paul himself might be read as doing so when he says that if Christ be not raised from the dead, then we are of all people to be pitied. Yet the Incarnation is far more mysterious than a resurrection. God, the transcendent Creator, Ruler, and Sustainer of the universe becomes a part of that creation. The resurrection, for which one should have a great deal of respect, still pales in miraculous significance to the Incarnation. The resurrection overcomes death. The Incarnation makes life.

I wrote earlier that miracles are sometimes understood as arguments for the reality of God. I also said that that view is faulty, for it misunderstands argument and reason. We can finally see why this is the case. If the Incarnation is the central truth of the universe, so that the Incarnation gives us the world itself, life itself, history itself, then how can a miracle, even an observed one, be evidence for the Creator? All creation is miraculous. Furthermore, reason and argument are taken as the touchstones for the true or the real. Reason points beyond itself, to hope and faith. What, then, is the connection between the miraculous and evidence? Some quotations from Pascal may enlighten us. He writes:

> Our religion is wise and foolish. Wise, because it is the most learned and firmly based on miracles, prophecies, etc. Foolish, because it is not all these things which make us belong. They certainly condemn those who do not belong, but do not make those who do belong believe. What makes them believe is the cross ... And so St. Paul, who came with wisdom and signs, said that he came with neither wisdom nor signs: for he came to convert. But those who come to convince can say they came with miracles and signs.[1]

Pascal elsewhere says:

> "If I had seen a miracle," they say, "I would be converted." How can they affirm what they would do about something of which they know nothing? They imagine that this conversion consists in worshipping God, seeing it as some kind of transaction or conversation. True conversion consists in self-abasement before the universal being whom we have so often angered and who could legitimately destroy us at any time, in recognizing that we can do nothing without him and that we have deserved nothing from him but our disgrace. It consists in knowing that there is an irreconcilable opposition between God and us, and that without a mediator there can be no transaction.[2]

Miracles, he says, "are the ultimate efforts of grace."[3]

Pascal's claim that miracles are things that make us belong, rather than believe, is of the utmost importance. Believing results from being convinced rather than being converted. Faith, in contrast, is a belonging, not merely a believing. Faith results from the cross, the event in history in which the Incarnate Lord takes on the suffering and death of humanity, the ultimate act of the Incarnation. We belong to the Creator as the divine takes on humanity. Faith flows out of the Incarnation of God, and the divine's very real, historical, crucifixion. On the cross, the nails went all the way through the human to God's own being. This is sacrament, the unity of the physical and the spiritual, God made manifest among us. At the crucifixion, the sacramental nature of Jesus is most clearly shown. Here God participates with us as the divine does no where else. God dies. Jesus himself is the outward sign of an inward grace, the lifting of everyday flesh into the glory that is God. That glory transforms the

---

1. Pascal, *Pensees*, 99.
2. Ibid., 92.
3. Ibid., 92.

flesh hung on the cross. History is never the same again, for all history is made holy in that moment. What Christ was by nature, we can now become by grace, as we participate in the transcendent reality made immanent in the very flesh of humanity.

The second quotation from Pascal notes, similarly, that some confuse the role of the miraculous, mistaking it for something leading to conversion. Such people take the miraculous as one side of a kind of transaction between God and humanity, the reasonable result of seeing a law of nature broken. God does the miracle, we respond by worshipping. Not so, says Pascal. Miracles may be able to convince, but they can not convert. Rather, conversion is self-abasement, the humility required of us all in our finitude before the majesty of God's being. Conversion is something we do, in the attitude of humility. We convert from thinking ourselves gods to thinking ourselves nothing without God. In short, in self-abasement we set aside our reasoning as the *only* path to truth, and, certainly, as the only path to life. This points again to the role of the Incarnation. The Word made flesh is a natural extension of God's creative work in speaking the world into being. At the core of that Incarnation is Christ's role as mediator between humanity and God.

So miracles are sacramental, outward and visible signs of inward and spiritual grace. Faith can see them, but don't ask miracles to provide evidence. Evidence is the wrong category. Evidence is a category of "pure reason." But reason isn't pure. Evidence can convince, but it cannot convert. To convert is an emotional, willful, and reasonable response to the God who far outstrips us in being.

But does understanding sacrament as the outward and visible sign of an inward and spiritual grace give us enough? What does it mean to say that? Let us begin again. The modern notion is that of a fixed world "out there." The radical postmodern notion is of fiction itself as "real." The former generates a skeptical chasm between reality and our beliefs, leaving us with the call for an existential leap to authenticity, and no more. The latter leaves us able to make things up and call it reality, letting us live in our fictionalities, our attempts to be God. Sacramentalism is the middle course, the history that begs to be lived. Sacramentalism struggles to hold the spirit and the body together. Heresies tend to split the two apart. The reality is, we cannot split asunder the body and the spirit. Reality is incarnational and, as such, our historical reality is sacramental. History and science need not be left alone, without meaning.

The empiricism embedded in the contemporary practice of history and science, while tending to leave reality out of reach, can be reunited with reality via the incarnational nature of Christianity. As such, creation, sacrament, crucifixion, and resurrection are all incarnational. But Christ must redeem history and science, for they cannot redeem themselves.

The Church catholic has seven sacraments: Baptism, Communion (Eucharist), Confirmation, Reconciliation of a Penitent, Unction, Marriage, and Holy Orders. In each of these, Christ is thought present in an incarnational way. Christ is present and presiding. Christ is incarnated and is, indeed, the grace received. The sacraments are "a sure and certain means by which we receive grace." Wholeness dwells here. No division of the physical and the spiritual crops up. The spiritual is infused in the physical. When we enter into the presence of the Eucharist, for example, we enter into the presence of Christ himself, the Incarnate one, who comes again in consecrated wine and bread. No mere physicality is suggested here, nor is there mere "symbolism," as if the bread and wine remain bread and wine. Once consecrated, the bread and wine are more than bread and wine. They are the body and blood of Jesus.

Other authors put this better than I. So consider Thomas Howard, in speaking of the Mass (Eucharist), the coming together for Communion. His emphasis is on the assembling of the people for Eucharist, but he cannot but burst out into the sacrament of Communion itself.

> The quality of being together has now been mantled with a mantle heavier than conviviality. This mantle, we might venture, partakes of the same flesh the Savior wore in His Incarnation. We are his Body. What can this mean? It is mystery, not to be dissipated by helpful talk of "body" suggesting mere togetherness, as in a metaphor. We have risen above the reach of metaphor here, to the realm of sacrament, where metaphor finally drops away, and meaning touches the actuality that the metaphor hints. In these precincts bread *is* (not recalls) the Sacred Body. Wine *is* (not signifies) the Precious Blood.[4]

The language begins to fail here. We are in the realm of sacrament, of mystery: *sacramentum* means "mystery." But it is mystery from our end, not God's. God can hold together the physical and the spiritual. We cannot. Every time we try, our theories come up with heretical undertones. Our epistemological abilities fall apart. Our beliefs and our reasoning

---

4. Howard, *On Being Catholic*, 87.

end up missing the mark. What we need is a view wherein truth reveals itself, an understanding in which truth is ontological rather than epistemological. God must reveal or we are surely lost. The sacraments are the means, sure and certain, by which we receive that grace, Christ himself made present.

"Anamnesis" is a term theologians use to get at the mystery. Surely Christ died once and for all on the cross outside Jerusalem. But in the Eucharist, Christ's death comes to us through anamnesis, the making present again what already happened. Although the crucifixion is historical, its influence is not "merely" historical. It is transformative. In the Eucharist as the priest consecrates the bread and wine, Christ himself is made manifest in his brokenness, suffering, and death. As we "feed on him spiritually in our hearts" his grace is imparted to us for repentance, renewal, and redemption. But it is Christ who we ingest, Christ who transforms us by being himself transformed, incarnated, to live among us. The living Spirit of Christ is made manifest again as flesh and blood, the wholeness of God among us.

Our greatest difficulty in seeing all this, of course, is our propensity to approach it all through the eyes of reason. Reason sees only two alternatives: One is that of the empirical, the modern. There are bodies in space, and they move about by mechanical control. No room for spirit exists here. We are left with the secular. The other is that of the radical postmodern, where we can simply cast into the minds of our imaginations and invent a story to live by. Both are heresies. Both leave us empty. Athanasius noted the first half of this problem long ago, and attributed it to the Fall. He wrote: "He [Christ] became himself an object for the senses so that those who were seeking God in sensible things might apprehend the Father through the works which He, the Word of God, did in the body.... When, then, the minds of men had fallen finally to the level of sensible things, the Word submitted to appear in a body, in order that He, as Man, might centre their senses on Himself, and convince them through His human acts that He Himself is not man only but also God, the Word and Wisdom of the true God."[5]

There is certainly a sense of humanity falling to the level of the sensible in this passage, yet no negative comment attaches to it. Athanasius is rather matter-of-fact about the situation. Indeed, humans are described as seeking God through the sensible. Not finding God there, God sends

---

5. Athanasius, *On the Incarnation*, 43, 44.

the divine more fully into the sensible so humans can do what they set out to do, viz., find God in the sensible. Hence the Incarnation. God was waiting for humanity finally to come to the place where they were seeking God *only* in the sensible. It was then, at that point in history, that Christ incarnated himself. Athanasius suggests that it was in the *human* acts of the Word that he was God, as well as human. Furthermore, the Word is incarnate so that the Word can center human senses on the Word as human. Notice it is the Word doing the centering, not humans themselves. God reaches us, not we God. In the Holy Sacrament that we call Jesus, we find the fullness of God's being. God enters history and redeems us. Reason alone cannot take us there. Emotions and passions alone cannot take us there. Will alone cannot take us there. Jesus must come to us.

But Jesus did not leave us alone when he returned to the Godhead. He gave us the sacraments of baptism, communion, holy orders, confirmation, confession, unction, and marriage in order for the Church to be the body of Christ. Jesus continues to be among us in incarnate form by his presence among us in history. Jesus is here. We need only open our eyes to see.

14

Virtue

Faith is sacramental. Faith is a belonging through the outward signs of an inward grace. As faith lunges toward the living Christ, we become aware of the reality of God incarnate in everything around us. We see the world anew as God is present in the creation.

Faith was not traditionally described as a sacrament but as a virtue. The Greek word we translate "virtue" is *arête*. *Arête* means both function and excellence. To ask for a thing's *arête* is to ask what its purpose is, and what its excellence is. The *arête* of a knife is to cut, and to cut excellently, with precision, ease, accuracy, and so forth. So when we speak of the virtue of a human, we must think of the function of a human and the excellence of a human. These are, frankly, more difficult to assess than they once were. The ancient Greeks held a teleological, goal-oriented understanding of humans. The advent of the mechanistic view of the universe, and later of the Darwinian-inspired theories in biology, tended to side-track the teleological view of humans. The influence of those positions in theology and philosophy are enormous. But if we are historical people, there is little denying that we think in terms of goals: for ourselves, our children, and our institutions or organizations. Still, the idea that humans have an "ultimate" purpose is difficult today for many to grasp. When we get much beyond the level of organization, perhaps to the level of culture or history, it is harder to see what an overarching goal would look like. Yet there are hints.

You have a lover. Your lover makes you very happy. Your lover, however, is unfaithful to you. Your best friend knows about the unfaithfulness. Would you rather your best friend tell you the truth and leave you living with the loss of the happiness or not tell you, and let you live with the happiness at the loss of the truth? I ask this question each term of my philosophy classes. It is rare to find people who disagree about which branch of this dilemma to take. The vast majority of people take the first branch of the dilemma, opting for truth over happiness.

Initially, these results suggest that attaining truth is more important to us than being happy. Yet in my discussions with people, I've discovered that their choosing truth over happiness hides an assumption. Most people also believe that in finding the truth, they will *eventually* find happiness. Attending this belief are the following corollaries—namely, that happiness based on an untruth is not real happiness, and that having the truth generates happiness. While the surveys I've conducted hardly constitute rigorous methodology, they are suggestive about human nature. We believe that truth and happiness are somehow linked. The question is, how?

Why do so many people believe that truth generates happiness, when no obviously necessary connection exists between the two? What if the truth about the world is horrible? For example, what if our entire experience in the world is delusory, so that most of our beliefs are false? Further, what if the actual truth about the world is that we are constantly suffering, and will for eternity? What happiness can be generated out of that truth? Having the truth does not necessarily link to happiness. Just as finding out that one's lover is cheating will make one unhappy, at least for a little while, finding out that the universe is a very unpleasant, painful place, and will be forever, will lead to a permanent unhappiness.

On the other side of the issue, perhaps happiness is just finding the truth and adjusting one's expectations to it. Happiness thus is nothing more than having an accurate perception of reality, no matter how bad reality is. Yet something seems awry here. Happiness is not merely some intellectual state. It involves the passions and perhaps the will too. While we can be happy in a state of pain temporarily, can we be happy without the possibility of hope? Again, hope looms large and seems necessarily positive and future oriented, indicating that we humans are incorrigibly goal oriented. As such, happiness dances in front of us, and we trust that truth will match our desire for a world that is capable of generating happiness.

We cannot shake the notion that humans are meant to be happy and that truth is ultimately, and ontologically, linked to happiness, even if we cannot show it to be such. But perhaps we are driven to this conclusion by too much Aristotelianism in our history. Two alternative ways of viewing the world in which happiness seems not to be the final goal are Zen Buddhism and Advaita Vedanta Hinduism. In both these views, but especially the former, the status of the self is not distinct. In Zen Buddhism, there is no self at all. In Advaita Vedanta Hinduism, *atman* is *brahman*; that is, the singular self is the universal self, leaving the nature of the human self indistinct from the universal reality. In both views, it fails to be clear whether happiness is a goal sought by the human being. Enlightenment in Zen Buddhism is the realization of the unreality of everything, and hence pain, as well as happiness, is illusory. There is, ultimately, no self to be happy. In Advaita Vedanta Hinduism, the self's goal is *moksha*: to be released from the cycle of reincarnation, so that the self is no longer individuated from ultimate reality. Again, the self cannot be said to have happiness as its goal, unless, of course, the uniting of the self with *brahman* is what defines happiness.

We cannot explore these religious and ontological views in depth here. It can still be said, however, that even if one holds these views, the goal of the "experienced" self to be free from the limitations of this world remains. So far forth, there is a goal-oriented understanding of the "self." In both cases, there are orientations toward the world. In Zen Buddhism, "one" seeks enlightenment and in the course of doing so, egolessness. Egolessness generates compassion. In Advaita Vedanta Hinduism, the singular self is enmeshed in the throes of karma and its moral and spiritual requirements. One is released in *moksha* only upon karma's demands being fulfilled. Both views treat other humans with moral respect, which in turn implies future orientation toward others and the world.

Furthermore, in Advaita Vedanta Hinduism, the goal of happiness stays on the horizon, for the self, while not distinguishable from the universal self in the final analysis, remains "involved" in reality. Hence, it's natural to think the self attains "happiness" upon its release from karma, even if that happiness is not "contained," so to speak, in a distinct self. The case of Zen Buddhism is more difficult. In what sense can happiness be the goal of a Zen Buddhist monk, seeking to be free from the illusions of the self? I said earlier that pain and happiness are illusory, but that was ill-spoken. Perhaps only temporal, this-worldly happiness is illusory. Could it not be said that insofar as the monk seeks freedom from the world that the monk seeks truth? In this case the truth is that there is nothing at all. But in that truth, the monk ceases to be, even as an illusion. So while temporal pain and happiness are not real, there remains a reality toward which the monk moves. That reality enables the cessation of the cycle of rebirth and freedom from illusion altogether. Isn't that, in some sense of the word, to be happy, where happiness is not the happiness of the self, of course, but the cessation of striving? Happiness turns out to be some sort of "feature" of reality, which is nothing.

To our ears, perhaps, this rings hollow. What is happiness, if not attached to a self? Perhaps I am trying too hard to make my point and retain the notion of happiness. Another tack suggests itself here. If the Zen Buddhists are correct, then happiness doesn't ultimately matter, for there is no self, indeed, there is nothing at all. The whole idea, then, of promoting compassion seems to make little sense, for if my self is illusory, then surely so are others. Without happiness as some sort of real possibility, morality seems to collapse as something that we should care about. Since Zen Buddhists care deeply about compassion, they also must care about the self and happiness. This, of course, is a point of logic and not a point of criticism about how Zen Buddhists actually live. Moral living may still flow in fact from a religious worldview, even if the metaphysics falls short of the true.

Barring the claims of Advaita Vedanta Hinduism and the even more rigorously anti-self Zen Buddhism, the desire for happiness seems built into human nature. We are goal oriented and it seems we are oriented toward happiness. But one must still admit that the connection between the truth and happiness isn't clear. In the final analysis, are happiness and truth the ultimate goals of human being? If they are not, what else could be? I do not know. I do know that our access to the notions that happiness is the ultimate goal of the human and that happiness is connected to truth seems rooted in hope. Here reason doesn't stand alone. It is natural to take our apparently in-built emotional attachment to these notions as an indicator of the direction to go.

What has all this to do with virtue? To understand what virtue is for humanity, we must understand the function of humanity. To understand function, we must understand nature. Are we by nature meant to be happy? Is that our purpose? While this cannot, I think, be proven, we nevertheless have the hints just rehearsed. Humans want to be happy, so we appear meant to be happy. What, then, makes us happy?

Humans are reasonable, emotional, and willful beings. Happiness for humans must recognize these features. It must be consistent with them. Thus, accessing the truth is important (and hence we have a pointer for linking truth and happiness), but the world must also be designed to recognize our emotions and will. Happiness cannot consist simply in recognizing the truth and adjusting our expectations to it, no matter how bad and how permanent. Dissatisfied with pain or suffering, we desire more. We hope things will get better. Indeed, we hope the universe is not ultimately unkind.

Enter faith. Faith is a virtue in that it strives to fulfill our goals of happiness. Even philosophical faith, with its ability to rest with the questions rather than answers, is a virtue. That is why the secular existentialists can take the authentic life to be one lived in the space of questions and uncertainty with openness to the future. But religious faith is more than that. It is a relationship to God. But such a relationship is sacramental. It is an outward sign of an inward grace. It is more than just convincement. It is conversion. Faith is a way of being in the world that recognizes our humility. It is a belonging. Thus faith shows itself in a life changed, a way of acting and working rearranged by the grace within. Faith cannot be separated from work, any more than the spiritual can be separated from the physical. Hence faith is not only a virtue but a sacrament.

Each of the sacraments has its own inward grace and its outward sign: Eucharist has the presence of Christ, Baptism has membership in the Church and water, Unction has spiritual and emotional healing and oil, and so forth. If faith is a sacrament, what is its inward grace, and what is its outward manifestation? For these things, we must look to work.

15

Work

Early on the third Sunday of Advent some years ago, I was on my living-room floor propped up on two large, blue pillows, lying on my right side. I was reading the part of *Walden* where Thoreau speaks of our lives of quiet desperation. Yet he states that the bedrock of reality remains a place to still our feet against the ravages of the news and begin our work anew. My head was resting uncomfortably on my right hand, the attached arm bent at the elbow. One of our four cats worked his nose into the crook of the joint.

I moved my fingers higher on my head to find a restful place when my thumb pressed hard on the flesh between my lips and cheek, and my other fingers pushed firmly at the soft area just beneath my eye and above the socket loosely gripping my eyeball. My thumb felt the ridge of bone running above my teeth, my fingers the ease with which my eye could be freed from my skull. I felt the deep connubial dance of flesh with bone, the coitus of shallow breath with skeleton. I sensed the work the union accomplishes—life with death; a sometime fast-paced jitterbug, an occasional unhurried ballet. And the other union, spirit and flesh.

What is work? The work of a hand is a revelation of life in a fleeting moment of touch. The feel of the flesh against bone, of sinew to foundation, rushes to fill my mind. I work each day. I am strong. I am fragile. Sometimes I work in strength. Sometimes I work in fragility. My work invigorates me. My work bores me. I see human culture in what I read. I read and my eyes get red and irritated. I see the new door frame in what

I cut. I look over the blade of the saw and the wood dust gets in my eyes. The work is redemptive. The work is cursed. What can Thoreau's walk around Walden pond teach me? What is the reality that forms the bedrock? Thoreau says we can return to spirit when the work is desperate. We can thus return to work anew. Yet, I suspect that returning to spirit so we can return to work is a false dichotomy.

The work I do is good, but the narrator in Ecclesiastes says that God has not given it to us to know the beginning and end of eternity. "Time is the stream I go a-fishing in," says Thoreau. I drink thirstily at it but see the thinness of its grasp on earth. And here I yearn to drink it all up! The stream bubbles, the earth groans. I strain to listen to what they tell. I garden on the banks of the stream, my back bent over the thoughts of other people, for I am a philosopher. There is a lot of poor soil around. But some good. How can I sort the good soil from the poor? But more to our point here, can I adjudicate spirit from flesh? No, Thoreau is wrong.

The Preacher says that all is vanity and nothing new exists under the sun. The news is not worth hearing. What profits it a person if a whole world is gained but the soul is laid up where moth and rust corrupts? How should we read this text? I am afraid that Christianity has been too corrupted to read this passage aright; Christianity's creeping Platonism corrupts it for us. I want us to remember that Christ died, after all, on a very wooden cross. We do not lay up our souls in Plato's realm of the forms. We lay them up in the world of tarts and tarragon. Christianity is a physical religion—souls are stitched to bodies inseparably. The bedrock is not a world of forms, not a world of spirit alone. It is a world of people, places, and epiphanies. It is a world of history and sacrament.

Thoreau is right when he tells us the work must begin anew, again. But it must be my work. It seems that the work others have done will not accomplish the task. Yet what is my work but theirs? My work is my culture, the world I spin out of our common imagination—blessed or cursed by God. My work is physical, the world I build out of my manual labor—good or bad. How can my work be truly mine; how can the physical work I do make a spiritual difference? By my work being the work of others. How can my work be their work? Via the work of Christ himself.

How can I gain an interest in my Savior's work? The physical work of Jesus on the cross accomplished a spiritual task. The building of corpuscle to corpuscle, of corpulent flesh to corpulent flesh, of rigid bone to rigid bone holds within it the spirit that is mine. The brick laying is tightly done. The work I do is what is killing me, but the work I do is of my nature. The redemption of the world is accomplished through the tearing of flesh from bone, my own an extension of others, and others an extension of the Maker's. The truth rests in the ongoing, never ending work of the earthworm, eating its way through miles of hard soil, passing its excretion into little, round black granules—worm casts rich in nutrients for plants to eat. The rotting remains of the Maker in the tomb becomes new life for us. The work was death but life as well. His body is not left there, but resurrected.

So with us. We work by the sweat of our brows and with us works Christ. When our head aches because of the din of the factory, his head aches because of the barbs of the crown. When our backs ache because of the weight of the load, his back aches under the lashing of the whip and the wood of the cross. When our hands and feet cry out in pain from the long walk and the repetition of the lifting, we must remember that his hands and feet cry out in pain as loud as the harmony of the universe rent asunder. We do not work alone.

I can learn much from Thoreau, but not that the hand is divided from the spirit; not that I should withdraw to Walden pond to reflect on "spiritual" things. We and our work are terrigenous. Redemption is work and therefore physical; it passes over a skull-shaped hill and through the rotting of the tomb. But work is redemption as well; the world can be reconstructed only through the physical.

Hence, the work one does is the outward sign of the inward grace that is faith. Work signifies the unity that is salvation. We work with our hands, mirroring God scraping together dirt to form us. We think, speak, and live, thus mirroring the creation of the world. We are faithful and virtuous in our jobs, with our friends, and with strangers seeking a cold cup of water. In short, we work out our faith with fear and trembling. We work out the truth in history. We can neither fall on the side of the spirit alone nor on the side of the physical alone, without falling into heresy. We must live in the space we call history, where God was incarnate and remains incarnate.

Yet something is left unspoken here. Evil, too, is incarnate.

16

Suffering

Suppose there is a good God, who is all-powerful and all-loving. God knows about pain and evil, and presumably wants to do something about them. Still, pain and evil exist. Whence suffering, if Christianity is true? Thus do many people set aside Christianity as implausible, if not impossible. Worth noting, however, is that evil, pain, and suffering don't thereby disappear. They just become nearly completely inexplicable and seemingly utterly pointless.

Facing the opposite direction, let's suppose Christianity is true. There is, therefore, an all-loving and all-powerful God who knows about evil and pain and wants to do something about them. Still, pain and evil exist, so there must be some sort of explanation for them that is compatible with what Christianity says about God. Evil, of course, doesn't disappear here either. But its inexplicability and pointlessness begin to shrink.

From the point of view of evidence, it is tempting just to set aside the issue as a draw. Christianity's critics will no doubt scream "foul," but why should they? If the Christian has some set of reasons to hold the faith, the issue turns on whether the evidence against theism provided by evil is strong enough to outweigh the evidence the Christian has for holding the faith. It is not as if the Christian ignores evil or suppresses its evidence. The problem of evil is not simply a logical issue from which one can distance oneself and thereby resolve neutrally. Evidence must be considered on all sides, including the inside, and so the Christian who believes there must be a solution to the problem of evil isn't being disingenuous, somehow suppressing the awareness of suffering.

Little is gained by leaving the problem of evil and pain on the merely intellectual level, for evil is not merely intellectual. Evil, pain, and suffering are also historical, touching us where we live, encroaching on everyone, Christians no less than those who are not. Indeed, evil and pain penetrate even the most ardent and faithful Christian. Indeed, Christians of all people should be most disturbed by evil, pain, and suffering. Pain, suffering, and evil made Jesus shed tears at the death of Lazarus. Jesus did not welcome the cross as if it would cause him no pain. To treat the problem of evil as if it were some sort of merely intellectual question is to miss the issue of pain. We *suffer* pain, we don't just think about it.

Philosophers often distinguish between evil and pain. In an earlier chapter, I noted the long history of understanding evil as a privation, a negation, an undoing of the good. This account of evil seems to suggest that evil doesn't exist. But that is to miss the point. Surely evil is real. But what is it, ontologically? If it is a privation, a lacking, then it is like a hole in the ground into which one may fall, or a hole in the wall of one's house through which blows the cold wind and rain. For being nothing, holes have rather important effects.

Whatever the exact status of evil philosophically, we know its influence in the world. Pain, whether physical or emotional, presses in on us. Some evil is freely done by moral agents, resulting in pain—philosophers call this "moral evil." Other evil comes about without the bad intent of any agent—what philosophers call "natural evil." Such evil also results in pain. In these latter cases, the pain itself just is the evil. A tree falling over in the rain and wind is a natural event. No one caused it. But when it falls on a child and smashes her skull open, the event is evil because of the pain.

Either way, whether pain is caused by moral intention or natural event, couldn't God have made the world in such a way that pain is unnecessary? So far as moral evil is concerned, philosophers have done a good deal of work on the so-called "free will defense." Roughly, the solution suggests that in order for certain good things to exist in the universe, God must allow humans to be genuinely free. In their genuine freedom, however, humans can choose to do bad things.[1] I, for one,

---

1. Plantinga, *God, Freedom and Evil*, and a good many others, provide excellent, technical analyses of the issues here. I grossly oversimplify some very technical philosophy.

think that the freewill defense is generally successful, and moral evil—the intentional harming of others—can be explained by the free actions of moral agents hence getting God off the moral hook. Furthermore, the natural events in the universe, such as rocks rolling down mountainsides, are not themselves inherently evil. So whether the event is intentional or not, God seems off the hook for what we think of as evil. But that doesn't explain pain, whether the pain results from bad moral intentions or comes about because a rock falls off the side of a mountain, crushing the legs of a young hiker.

I want to narrow the discussion to pain, as over against evil *per se*. Pain itself, whether it be the negative (physical) sensations we feel when we cut ourselves by accident or the negative emotional pain we experience when someone treats us unjustly, is bad. Indeed, pain is quintessentially bad. No one seeks pain because it is good. Although we might be willing to undergo some pain (e.g., a surgery) in order to bring about something better, no one chooses pain because he or she enjoys it.

Why couldn't God have made the world in such a way that we don't feel pain? Some have suggested that pain is justified because it is a warning system that helps keep us from harm. Well, why didn't God just put something in our brains so that when our bodies are in danger, we simply pull back? Why does pain have to register? It might be suggested that given our human nature (and for that matter, non-human animal nature too), pain receptors in our nervous systems are the most efficient way to get our attention when we are in physical danger. But even were this true, no explanation is forthcoming to indicate why we suffer emotional pain. Emotional pain often doesn't warn us off some danger. Depression, bi-polar disorder, schizophrenia, and other mental conditions, even emotional states such as grief, discouragement, or sadness, don't enable us to move out of harm's way, like a burnt finger moves us away from the open flame. Perhaps we can say that the capacity for happiness requires the capacity for sadness, perhaps even the capacity for mental illness. If we are not able to grieve the death of a loved one, perhaps we are not able to have loved ones, for we can't love at all. To love is, perhaps, to grieve.

Be all that as it may, I want to focus even more narrowly on a peculiar type of pain. I want to think together about suffering. Suffering goes beyond mere pain. Although we can say things like "he suffered a short pain when he jabbed the pin into his finger," I have in mind suffering in the extended sense. Some people develop chronic disorders such as lupus, Parkinson's, or diabetes. Others become ill with slow moving, but incurable cancers, or AIDS, or other painful illnesses. Finally some are born with the frustrating challenges of cerebral palsy or ALS, where one's mind is fine, but the body won't cooperate. Each of these is painful either physically, emotionally, or both. The pain doesn't go away. Suffering is relentless, often permanent pain, more or less excruciating. If it is not permanent, it is ongoing long enough that one can't tell the difference between excruciating and not. Suffering more often than not brings the suffering person to the point of wishing for death to be free of the pain.

Such pain affects not only the person directly receiving it, but also loved ones closely attached to the sufferer. Not only does a daughter weep in her lung cancer, but her parents look on with tears running down their faces and directly into their hearts. Suffering affects those around it. This brand of pain has no justification in terms of warning us off something bad. Suffering is at the core of the problem of evil. How much, exactly, is enough?

I wrote a poem about me and my late wife, who suffered with and from lupus, Raynald's syndrome, interstitial cystitis, Sjogren's syndrome, and other disorders, none of which are curable, all of which are painful, and none of which ever went into remission for her. She had chronic bladder pain, more or less like a severe bladder infection that never went away. Many of her joints ached constantly. She lost her ability to balance herself well. Her mucus membranes and her skin dried out, sometimes cracking and bleeding. Her hands burned and itched. She had any number of other pains as well. She had chronic headaches. A not atypical week consisted of spending four of the five weekdays in doctor's offices, labs, and hospitals. A friend of hers with lupus called it the "pain du jour." We thought that eventually some complication from these diseases would kill her. There was little hope that she would ever live without pain. One day, when she was convinced, apparently, that her life was so negatively affecting my older son's and my life, she took her own. Obviously, her illnesses affected me and our family. She could do very few domestic chores, and her ability to work was extremely limited, although she managed through Herculean effort to teach half time. Finishing her PhD dissertation was a pipe dream. The following poem expressed how suffering affects two married people (leaving out our son), both of whom loved each other deeply.

Martyrs

And so it runs,
the long, slow, suffering
death of someone I love
slipping through the petals of
life, too young to die but
dying anyway. Her dreams
crushed, her plans
gone, her life lived behind the
mask. Where is thy sting, O death,
where is thy sting?
It's here, on our porch, where her
plants, once so well-tended, lay prostrate for
lack of drink. Another task I should
have done, but didn't.
It's here, in the sink, where the
tower of dishes leans over the edge, unable to
bear another cup for fear of collapsing onto
the dirty floor. Another task I should
have done, but didn't.
It's here, on the floor, where last
week's newspapers lay strewn about, waiting
for someone to bring order to their stories.
Another task I should have done,
but didn't.
It's hard to live two lives,
where only one should be.
But this isn't about pity, please.
It's about us, together. Her death is near
to mine. And the two shall become
one flesh, so says the book we quoted and
believed.
We didn't know two flesh
could be crammed into such
a small space.
Her death is near
to mine. In sickness and in
health, says the liturgy we uttered and
believed. At eighteen and twenty-one, who thinks
of sickness?
We didn't know that old age can begin
at thirty, and that health is something that
fails even when life is still arousing.

> Her death is near
> to mine. Til death do you part,
> says the story for love we cried our way through that
> day in Woodland Hills. Death, we thought, happens
> once.
> We didn't know that death can slowly oxidize any good
> metal, even gold.

This is a hint of shared suffering. I must say that I didn't feel her pain. Her pain was hers; her suffering hers. In fact, I'm not one to jump into pain voluntarily. I've seen too much of her suffering, and seen too many of her goals and plans not just wither, but burn up in the sun. As much as I'd like to say I bore her suffering, I don't believe it for a minute. Oh, I bore some burdens for her. I spent a good deal of time doing things for her that a healthy person could have done for herself. Some of the things I'd like to have done, whether with her or without her, went undone. Vacations were nearly impossible. I suppose during the ten years of her suffering I could have written more and made more of a name for myself in the academic world. But these are minor things compared to the day in and day out, night in and night out, sufferings that she bore. And to what end?

What was and continues to be especially difficult for me is the sense that she suffered so that I would become a more loving person. That is a burden I don't like to think about, but I believe it is a burden she carried nevertheless. There is a deep mystery here. We are once again in the realm of sacrament. Here our marriage, my being a priest, unction, and a host of other sacramental things come together. At the heart of Christianity beats the heart of a Savior who suffered with all of humanity's sickness, sin, and guilt. It was a heart literally pierced with a soldier's spear. This outward sign became an inward pain. That pain was somehow transformed into grace, itself transforming humanity from weak, sinful, fallen creatures into brothers and sisters of the Ruler of the universe.

The Christian doctrine of the communion of the saints is often overlooked, but is essential to even a rudimentary grasp of Scripture as it tells us to fulfill the sufferings of Christ. The Church, we are told, is Christ's body. When one part suffers, we all suffer. So when Christ dies on the cross, we all die, and we are all resurrected as he is. When one of us suffers, she suffers for all humanity. I dare not claim to understand this mystery, but the offering up of one's suffering to the recipient Lord of Hosts contributes to the salvation of the world. This is what suffering means.

Yet I take no pleasure in it. Treating suffering lightly, without deep tears and agony in the stead of our suffering sisters and brothers, cheapens the reality of that suffering. Grace does not come without a great price. Neither does God take pleasure in suffering. We don't worship a cosmic sadist. Nor is God a masochist. But evil, pain, and its concomitant suffering exist. God does not stand watching on the side of the rushing river watching someone drown while wringing the divine hands as if not knowing how to swim. God incarnates into the very middle of the social, political, moral, and natural evil, thereby redeeming it.

Our suffering too is taken by our brother Christ and transformed into grace. An old use of the term "suffer," one we don't take advantage of much any more, is "to receive an image." For a piece of wax, metal, or wood to suffer, is for it to bear an image. So for a human to suffer is for that person to bear an image—the image of Christ himself. This image of the one who shaped the universe is also the image of a sufferer who bore our image of weakness, sin, sickness, and death. In our suffering, we transform others, and perhaps, too, ourselves.

I am beyond hesitant to say the typical thing here, viz. that a severely deformed baby is born so the parents can learn to love. These things cannot be spoken in abstract. Just as there must be a name attached to a moral judgment,[2] so there must be a name attached to a judgment about suffering. It is too easy to generalize (sometimes with cruelty, although unintentional). People say that just as Mary and Joe's son was born with spina bifida in order that Mary and Joe would grow closer to God, so all suffering of this sort finds its reason in friends and relatives growing closer to God. There are just as many parents who develop a deep suspicion of God, hope, love, or faith, while watching their child grow up in suffering. I do not believe these things can always be balanced in some direct way, that this child's suffering saves this parent. The work of suffering is both greater and deeper than that. But it is important to recognize a point of logic, which is, simply put, that anyone *can* learn from his or her *own* suffering. But this must be something pronounced with great caution. Whether any one actually *does* learn must only be reported personally and not from the outside. Such descriptions require autobiography. Too many well-meaning people say, "hang on, it will be OK," when the appropriate response is to weep with the sufferer.

2. See comments by Hallie, "From Cruelty to Goodness."

Suffering cannot be understood externally. Indeed, many people who suffer refuse to say that they understand it. How can it, therefore, be understood by an outsider? But Christ connects us to the inside of his story and encourages us to suffer his image. Such suffering is what we are called into, Christian or not. How we respond is up to us. The bodily and emotional suffering we take on is not good, and we should never confuse it with good. Yet the Christian believes the love of God is so powerful that even evil, pain, and suffering can be transformed. God's being is beyond us in goodness and power. What God can bring about is, finally, a mystery.

Evil is historical, and we are historical people. We live in the space between fiction and objectivity. How we deal with evil is also something that we live. We interpret evil just as we interpret all the other events in our lives. Whether there is a God who loves us cannot be determined solely on the grounds of evil, for evil itself can be imbedded in a story that helps us live with it, or evil can be left on its own without God, and we can bear it on our own. Yet the hope that love can conquer suffering is a powerful antidote to the loneliness that evil makes us suffer. The issue is whether we can suffer the image of love to mold us. But it is essential that we name evil and suffering accurately. There is no room to make suffering into something light or unimportant. Suffering must be called what it is, evil. But having named it what it is, we must work toward its end.

Just a few days after his mother died, Ian and I were at his uncle and aunt's home, camping in the backyard. We were trying to sleep when he asked why? Why did mom die? Did God do this?

These words came from my lips, but I suspect their source was divine: "The universe has evil and suffering in it. Denying God's love and existence on the basis of evil is not irrational. But a universe with God and evil is a lot less lonely than a universe with just evil."

I think that is true.

17

Reality

IF THERE IS A single text that has influenced me most deeply outside of Scripture, it is the myth of the cave. In Plato's *Republic*, Socrates is asked to explain the Good. Socrates replies that he cannot give a *logos* (a reasoned account), but only a *mythos* (a story). What a revelation! When Plato searches for other bits of truth, it is the *logos* of a thing he seeks. But when pursuing the question of the Good, the most important of all essences, Plato responds with the myth of the cave, the story of the sun, and the analogy of the divided line. Although the truth is within us, we cannot find the truth by ourselves. We need a guide. This is at least hinted at in the myth of the cave, where Plato describes what might happen to someone who has seen the Sun (the Good) but who returns to the cave to help free others from their blindness and their bindedness.

Jesus, too, says the kingdom of God is within us. Once again, we are not left alone without a guide. A community of Christians exists, not all of whom are gifted guides, but many of whom are. This community reflects the Eternal and Holy Trinity, consisting of the Third Person of the Trinity, the Holy Spirit, who Christ promised as Guide and Comforter, the Second Person, the Lord Christ himself, the Way, the Truth, and the Life, and the First Person, the Creator and Sustainer, the Mother and Father of us all. These three together, are autobiographers, *par excellence*. Not only do they contribute interpretations, but they also supply the basic building blocks. They are also historians, recording *our* stories. But the Persons of the Trinity are not the "objective" historians of the modern world. They participate with us in our lives. Our histories and their autobiographies get run together. Far from being objective in their reading and telling of the stories, they are right in the mix. Perhaps we might think of the Holy Three as the Grand Revisionist Historians of our lives. Not only can they rewrite our lives when we get off the path, they can do so from the inside, as those who research and live the history—they are auto-historians.

Where is reality in all this? Frankly, it's not as clear or as accessible as we might wish. We tend to think of reality as something "out there" that our subjective persons have access to via the means of empirical information. But we sense, as did the moderns, a gap between what is out there and what we know. How do we get the "out there" "in here?" The modern answer leads, I think, to skepticism. The radical postmodern answer is to simply "make it up," to fictionalize it all. But both the modern and the radically postmodern are heretical. The trick is to keep the physical and the spiritual together, whole, complete, without falling onto one side or the other.

An interesting phenomenon is found among the mystics. Certain mystical experiences lead the mystic to complete certainty of the reality she or he experienced. Indeed, the reality is often spoken of as more real than ordinary empirical things. Among Christian mystics is found an inkling of the explanation for this certainty.[1] In what are called "full union" mystical experiences, Christian mystics tell us that although they are not united with God in being (that would mess up the Christian theological account of God and humans as separate kinds of beings), they are united in will. God's will simply becomes their will. In wondering about this, I considered what we have certainty about in our non-mystical lives, if anything. If we are certain about anything, we are certain about our own internal psychological, emotional and willful states. I know that it *seems* cold to me. I know that I am angry. I know that I wanted to win the election.[2] These are "subjective" in one sense. They are internal to our minds. Nevertheless, they are no less real or "objective" than other features of the universe. It is an objective feature of the universe that now

---

1. Certainty is also reported among mystics who are not Christians as well. However, I think theists have the best chance of explaining this certainty, for the theology and ontology appears to be in place to do so, as I suggest below.

2. There are borderline cases here. I may not always be sure of my emotions or my willings. But there are paradigm cases too, and it is the paradigm cases of psychological certainty that I have in mind.

I feel a pain in my lower left back, just below the rib cage. Yet my access to that fact is subjective and always so.

The Christian mystic reports that God's will becomes the mystic's will, and surely this would *feel* for the mystic just like he or she is God. So, if in reality God's will becomes the mystic's will, then the mystic will be as certain of God's existence and reality as the mystic is of his or her own existence and reality. That brings the "out there" "in here," bridging the modern's gap. This observation points us in the direction of a path between the modern and the radical postmodern, where things are neither completely empirical nor completely fictional. Reality is internalized externality. The mystic, for a few brief moments, shares the will of God. What is external to the mystic—God—becomes internal to the mystic. But while this phenomena appears limited to the handful of mystics having full union experiences, the theology (and hence ontology) of it is not.

St. Paul, in writing to the Colossians, says: "Now I rejoice in what was suffered for you, and I fill up in my body what is still lacking in regard to Christ's afflictions, for the sake of his body, which is the church. I have become its servant by the commission God gave me to present to you the word of God in its fullness—the mystery that has been kept hidden for ages and generations, but is now disclosed to the saints. To them God has chosen to make known among the Gentiles the glorious riches of this mystery, which is Christ in you, the hope of glory."[3]

Christ in you, the hope of glory. The reality of the Gospel is that Christ is in us. Our task is to pay attention to this internalized externality. As we do, we are able to live our lives historically, with God the Mother-Father, God the Son, and God the Holy Spirit living and writing our histories along with us. We can be transformed into the people God wants us to be, without falling prey to modern or postmodern heresies.

Yet reality is not, I think, just internalized externality but externalized internality. There is a role, and a large one, for our thoughts and language (our conceptual schemes or perspectives) to make the world. The future is open and we shape it not merely by our decisions but also by the way and via the terms in which we think. So we carry what is typically thought of as internal to the external. We make the world. And if there are competing ways in which the world is because of competing conceptual schemes, then the world is many, conflicting ways. But these

---

3. Col 1: 24–27 NIV.

ways are not so wildly conflicting that morality and theism are lost. In fact, we need God in all our conceptual schemes to make sense of the laws of logic, the truth of morality and the very existence of our own creative persons.

Reality is the space between the empirical and the fictional. But it is a space where God most definitely must be, and where Christianity was, is, and shall be. We cannot escape our own historicity, nor can we escape the historicity of the God who is eternally Three in One and One in Three and yet also the God who incarnated the divine self through the Son, and who sends the Holy Spirit to dwell within us. We must all tell our stories, and live our histories. In doing so, we live our autobiographies. What you've read so far is largely autobiographical. In the preface to *Orthodoxy* Chesterton wrote, speaking of his book, that "it is unavoidably affirmative and therefore unavoidably autobiographical."[4] I hope thus far I have been affirmative. I know I have been autobiographical. But I hope the path is wide enough so you can join me.

But if I began writing this book thinking of autobiography, it was natural for me to begin by thinking of apology. As I was growing up, I felt a more or less acute embarrassment at being a Christian. Many of my friends were not Christian and, indeed, little that went on in my church helped me figure out why Christianity is true. Further, my embarrassment at the Gospel was ingrained into me, whether consciously or not, by those around me. Christians were, well, sort of odd or unusual. The idea wasn't so much that we Christians had crazy ideas (although that may be true too), but rather that we were a peculiar people, a malapropos mob.

Later, when I began college and began to study apologetics (the defense of the faith) I was happier, but still found the approaches off-putting and distant, too abstract to connect with the skepticism I felt. As I matured and found myself buried in the mystery that is the Trinity, I realized that to become a real apologist, one has to be stuffed with bread and crocked with wine. The outward signs must become the inward graces, stuffed and crocked. But bread is to be shared, and the purpose of wine isn't to remain crocked in some corner by yourself, or to leave the bottle corked. The purpose to be uncorked and poured out as a libation, a living sacrifice, so others can be crocked as well.

Today, I wonder if my early feelings of embarrassment weren't so far off, but rooted in some pre-reflective awareness that apology isn't

---

4. Chesterton, *Orthodoxy*, vii.

about a defense against intellectual attack (Christians always seem to need an enemy) but rather about being sorry. I'm sorry the gospel is offensive. I'm sorry you (we) don't like it. But there it is, the truth spoken out loud. Christians *are* a peculiar people. I wish we were more peculiar, for how would the world look if all Christians really laid down their lives for their friends?

Sacramentalism struggles to hold the spirit and the body together. Sacramentalism is at the center of the Christian faith. Heresies tend to split off one aspect from the other. The reality is, we are both spiritual and physical; spiritually earthy, and earthily spiritual. The path toward reality is the path that allows us to dance with the Holy Trinity, between the extremes of empirical emptiness and fictionalized make-belief. In this space we call history, we find the living God, and while we shed our blindness, we don't completely shed our bindedness. Instead, we renew it by living it out through the tradition that is the Church catholic, with all its richness and wooing toward the Reality of the One who loves us and lives among us.

In some ways, this book is over. I have attempted to explain my central thesis, and the book could be set aside here. Yet some thoughts linger. They don't seem to fit directly into the narrative. Some details are more explicitly autobiographical than much of what you've read so far. So, I've included them, and I invite you to read on. In them, you'll see many of the themes I've discussed, along with some new ones. But perhaps more importantly you'll see some peculiarities of a few of the people in my life who've called themselves Christian, along with some more of my own peculiarities. I've tried to embrace them all, and in so doing, to live my life in integrity, between the heresies. To how much success, others will have to judge.

18

Voice

GRANDDAD HAD A GRAVELLY voice. It scared me when I was a boy. As I grew, so did his voice. At first it was the distant rumble of the train two township roads over, toward the limestone quarry. Later it was a nearby roar. The roar wasn't more clear than the rumble, though more effective. Such a voice must, I thought, be rooted in anger. Still young, I couldn't distinguish anger and love. His warning words growled me down from the wood pile and away from the careless use of the axe.

Granddad was quiet. He spoke only when spoken to. He spoke in short sentences. He worked, when I was a boy and he a late-middle-aged man, in Long's foundry. The noise of the machinery bade Granddad keep quiet. A few of his friends and my father called him "Hewy." My grandmother never did. His real name was Elgin. I don't know the origin of the nickname; it harbors in the mists of the past beyond the foundry. To my mind, it never fit Granddad. The word was onomatopoeic, not naming Granddad but describing his voice. When my father called Granddad "Hewy," the pronunciation seemed to clear Dad's throat of foundry dirt and dust, as if the voice he described were shaped by the work its owner was forced to do. Granddad's voice was muffled during his foundry years. The machines couldn't hear him anyway, except for the occasional "goldamned thing." I never heard stronger language from him.

Before the foundry, and long before he knew me, he was a farmhand on the old Turnbull place. Some work was done with neighbors, but a man is often alone on a farm. He spent many quiet hours, with only the cows to listen as he milked the early mornings away. Cows will listen, but understand a warm hand as well as a voice. After he retired from the foundry, the farm became his home again. Not the big farm, but the place on which stood the old schoolhouse where he'd attended as a boy. He began to talk. Or I began to listen. He told stories of the old farm days and community gatherings, complained about the government's interference in farming, and spun out the ever-larger tale of his life. He rarely spoke of the foundry.

On a Christmas visit in 1990, after I had stopped eating meat because of the poor treatment of the factory farm animals, I thought my grandfather would be upset by my "crazy California ideas." I worried about my possible need to refrain from the generosity of the table at Christmas. Granddad was of an older generation. I thought he wouldn't understand, while my parents would more easily live with my decision. I was wrong. Granddad's years on the small farms, and his constant following of agricultural trends pushed on farmers by the government, lent to Granddad a sympathetic ear. His work surprised me once again. The stories of his life were molded by his work, especially the stories of his youth.

The old days were keen as he spoke of his childhood neighbors, many still living on or near their farms in the midst of which stood his beloved schoolhouse. The Cairns, the Whitneys, the Gowanlocks, the Browns, and the Brennans; all neighbors willing to work together to bring in the hay, rent a pasture, or pull a car out of the ditch on stormy winter days so someone could get to work in town. Granddad knew them all. Even those no longer too nearby. When asked, he'd stretch his memory to think of who lived where and when, how it came to be that the farm turned hands, and why the drifting of neighborliness left the landscape bare. He and his brother-in-law Randy talked for hours, half the year in the porch screened to keep at bay the flies drawn by the farm's sun-warmed manure and the other half in the wood stove's heat cast into the kitchen. Both farmers, they ruminated about changes in the local geography and the neighbors who changed with it.

The farm was not Granddad's first love of place. That was left for the bush. He wouldn't exactly disappear without telling Granny where he was going, although he might have had he thought he could get away with it. Precedent stood against him. Granny's father used to disappear into the bush without notice to my great Granny B., who often went about the old Boynton farmhouse gnashing her teeth at being left alone. Granddad dare not think of failing to voice his bushward intentions.

But to the bush Granddad went. The fever started just when the first pieces of hard wood were lifted into the fireplace in late fall, chasing the morning's deep frost. "I've got to get to the bush," he'd mutter. He felled the old-stand maples, oaks, and other hard woods to be cut and hauled, eventually to cure, for husbandry in the fire a winter or two away. In other work, Granny and Granddad returned to the tools of an earlier generation—a hand churn, a hand-cranked whetstone, a woodstove—but Granddad used a chain saw to cut wood. I'm sure Granddad understood that chainsaws were not antiques. Still, the inconsistency was a minor one, and Granddad wasn't against power tools in principle. He simply thought the old ways were good ways. But the wood had to get cut, and he was an expert. After Granddad had some heart trouble, my older brother helped split some wood. Phillip picked up the axe as Granddad placed the condemned piece of wood facing just so. Pointing to this knot or that spot, Granddad encouraged Phillip to strike the blow as instructed. Phillip was amazed at Granddad's ability to pick the spot on the wood to make the splitting more easy. More easy, not ever reposeful, for wood that stands in place hundreds of years bent under the force of the wind doesn't quit without an argument. After noting to me the difficulty of the work, Phillip added that Granddad left the harder wood for himself to split. Mixed with his blood was the tiniest trace of oak-tree sap; enough to make him stubborn, and just enough to hold his body together for eighty-three years.

Or perhaps it was a trace of sugar-maple sap in his blood. After selling off a piece of land held with his cousin Mel, the closest thing to a bush Granddad owned was the half acre or so of sugar maples on the schoolhouse property. During Easter recesses when I was ten or eleven or so, my younger brother Art and I would go to Granny and Granddad's to work carrying the overflowing buckets of sap up to the large pans set low on rocks over what would become, around supper, the fires magically turning the sap to maple syrup. Granddad worked diligently and quietly late into the evening, tending the hardwood fires. The first syrup of the year was always the sweetest, except when Granddad let the fires get too hot and that golden nectar burned. Granny complained, not always with a twinkle in her eye, about how Granddad always burned the first batch.

Words were often a more-or-less one way street with Granddad and Granny. She is a strong woman. But love was always a country road, narrow, but with room for both to pass. Their love always struck me as ancient, as if it had no beginning. The mystery is a good one. Some loves, though beyond our ken, support us. Although Granddad had a temper, he never struck Granny. She speaks fondly of a time, shortly after they married, when they finger wrestled. She won. After this defeat, he raised his arm against her in humiliation. He didn't strike. Sensing too much the likeness to the motion of an axe, he let his arm fall loose. Red ragged, he charged out of the room. Later he returned, flowers in hand. Rarely did he voice his sorrow, but the flowers quietly appeared. She knew. He never raised his arm to her again.

The flowers he brought were frequently fresh-picked from the bush. My family, Granddad, and Granny went often to walk among the trees in the spring warmth, the moss spongy beneath our feet and the flowers embroidering the open meadows. Once, when I wasn't more than five or six, we went to pick morels. On this occasion I first grew cognizant of Granddad's knowing love of the bush and of me. He and I struck out together in one direction, hand in hand, all eyes turned to the earth. I saw a brown and beige waffled bulge on the ground. Not knowing its name, I asked him. Granddad grumbled out, "that's a morel—now look for more. Where there's one, there's two." Morels will for me forever symbolize community and family.

Beside the wood, the flowers, and the morels, blueberries constituted the bush's generous offerings. Granddad and Randy spent days poking around the bush near Port Stanton, covering the stretches of flat rock entangled by blueberry bushes. Next to cutting wood, picking blueberries was, I suppose, Granddad's favorite task. The simplicity of receiving the bounty of God from nature, the honor, honesty, and goodness of the work made my grandfather who he was. I worked in my father's shoe repair shop at fifteen, and we put new soles and heels onto a pair of Granddad's shoes. When he came to pick them up, I explained to him that there was no charge. Ten minutes later he left, finally convinced that he need not pay. He never relished the thought of taking the result of another person's labor without returning its worth. He thought nothing, in turn, of leaving without charge, farm-fresh eggs, butter, and milk for friends and neighbors, in need or not. The bounty of the bush and of neighborliness taught him this generosity.

Love filled Granddad at home, on the farm, and in the bush, but the church focused his actions. He ushered on Sunday mornings into his eighties, his warm smile beaming to new and old. His quiet manner suited his servant-like work. My discovery of it was the morning I was baptized at fourteen. He was in one of the old First Baptist Church building's Sunday school classrooms (with the walls that pulled up from the floor!), missing the worship service, to make sure that the boys being baptized got into the right spot at the right time. His eyes shone then just as they did when he met my ten-month-old son nearly twenty years later. New life always brought that shine. If his mouth didn't speak, his eyes did.

Toward the end of his life, a stroke disabled Granddad. His once gravelly voice turned even lower and seemingly gruffer, the words harder to make out. My (now late) wife and I talked about my calling him over the phone from California, but I didn't want him to be embarrassed by my old inability to sort out his words. Or perhaps I didn't want to be embarrassed. I thought then of why I couldn't understand him when I was a child. Was it inattention? Was it my own childhood speech impediment? I now think not. Rather I think my early disability allowed me to love him more deeply than otherwise. His words were few. They spoke only of what he knew, the farm and the bush, neighbors and family. Although his voice was not often heard, I knew him well. Whatever words he spoke, he stood by them.

For all the integrity of his words, his work stood for his character; a voice louder and clearer than any vibration of vocal chords. Granddad worked hard all his life. At the funeral, as friends, neighbors, and family passed by the casket and shook hands with Granny, my uncles and mother, all the grandchildren, and some of the great grandchildren, one could almost predict what each would say. The one who spoke the clearest, though, was a Mr. Chambers. He knew Granddad when he was eighteen and Chambers was ten. The bond between them must have been strong, for Chambers had to introduce himself to the family, never having met any of us, including Granny. Mr. Chambers hadn't seen Granddad in sixty-five years. He said two things: Elgin was quiet and Elgin worked hard.

On the Monday before Granddad died, my mother visited him in the hospital. He sat in a chair for the first time since the stroke, his head dangling over like a slightly wilted daffodil. His paralyzed foot touched the floor, unable to feel the cool linoleum. The presence of the stroke's results became real. A great sadness in his words, Granddad voiced the end of his life: "My working days are over." But he need not be sad anymore. I like to think that when Granddad died, God needed a bushman, a simple woodcutter. I like to suppose that as Granddad walks and works among those resurrected trees, carrying and using his saw, that his voice is the clearest and his work a most marvelous pastime, for he sings with the angels.

One has little control over the places of one's life. The landscape induces one to be of one culture rather than another, to be of one place rather than another. My grandfather was of the culture of neighborliness rather than of transit; he was of small-town farm community rather than cityscape distance. With gentle work one afternoon, two of my cousins, my two brothers, my brother-in-law, and I set Granddad's casket into the vault. It was a warm April day, a breeze billowing the spring's wild May flowers so-loved by Granddad. We walked away quietly. Later that day I flew into Chicago to interview for new work. The city smell invaded me. Still, Granddad's life lingered in my thoughts. He would have enjoyed a visit there, but the noise and traffic, the crowds and the skyscrapers, would have eventually driven him home to his farm and his bush. Two days later I rode the Northern local, fitting in a visit with my old college friend Cody and her kids, living in a north shore Chicago suburb. She had grown up there, lost her father, graduated, married, divorced, married, moved to Texas, had a child, divorced, returned, graduated college, married, had a child, divorced, waitressed, took care of her mother, became a teacher, lost her mother, and continued to struggle to raise her two kids. The two-story, insulbrick-sided houses, lining the railroad tracks between downtown and Cody's home, standing in rows between the small factories and warehouses, reminded me of the oddness of geography's influence in our lives. Granddad would have been a person of another kind had be been born here and not in northern Orillia township. Had he been buried in the graveyard beside the railroad tracks, between the factories, instead of the gentle hillside next to my long-dead uncle Art's grave, would he have turned into a different kind of dust?

A few days later, I spoke to Granny long distance from California. Torn between selling and keeping the schoolhouse as almost sixty years of living with the woodcutter began to drift away from her, I was again aware of the voice of work and place. Granny needed to live in their place and among their work, at least for a time. Granddad was not easily separable from the wood piles and maple trees. In time, by working at the place, Granny would become restful again, able to say farewell to Granddad, without having his place, his work, his memory, wretched from Granny's hands. His voice would fade from the geography but come home to her.

Two months later I got the work I'd rushed away to Chicago for. The interview at the convention went well. The University of Texas and San Antonio became my family's new place. After almost fifteen years in Southern California, the geography shifted again. Just as I almost became at home. Would that I could sit in Granny's rocker, moving in place, viewing my life's work, without another move.

19

Sexism

For whatever reasons, good and bad, I have been unwilling until now to open in myself what I have known all along to be a wound—a historical wound, prepared centuries ago to come alive in me at my birth like a hereditary disease, and to be augmented and deepened in my life . . . . This wound is in me, as complex and deep in my flesh as blood and nerves. I have borne it all my life, with varying degrees of consciousness, but always carefully, always with the most delicate consideration for the pain I would feel if I were somehow forced to acknowledge it. But now I am increasingly aware of the opposite compulsion. I want to know, as fully and exactly as I can, what the wound is and how much I am suffering from it. And I want to be cured; I want to be free of the wound myself, and I do not want to pass it on to my children.

—Wendell Berry[1]

BERRY'S PICTURE AND UNDERSTANDING of White racism against Blacks in the United States and its effects on both Blacks and Whites is one of the most true that I know. Therefore I want to apply his insights to another problem. I know of such a wound in me, and I want to be cured. My wound too is as deep as blood and nerves in my flesh. The wound is layered over with well-meaning intentions and false generosities. So deep is the wound that although I've known it was there nearly all my life and although I've spoken of it in public many times, I feel I am only now

---

1. Berry, *Hidden Wound*, 3, 4.

beginning to be aware of it. And I want to be cured; I want to be free of the wound myself, and I do not want to pass it on to my children.[2]

My wound is the result of sexism, and like racism's negative effect on both Blacks and Whites, sexism negatively affects both women and men. I hasten to add that I don't want to deny or obfuscate the darkness of the hurt women have faced at the hands of violent men. Physical and sexual abuse done to women by men is rampant in all classes of North American society and world-wide. Such horrific things I wish everyone desired to eliminate. I do not want to, nor will I, minimize the harm done to women who receive violence from men. Yet it remains to ask what harm is done to the men who hold women in such contempt. What harm is done to the men themselves in acting in these violent ways and what harm was done to these men in the past that allows them to do such harm to women in the present?

Sexism is not ended merely by stopping male violence against women. Sexism wields power much more subtlety than overt acts of physical and sexual abuse themselves suggest, for deep emotional and spiritual components root sexism. Not all men are violent toward women physically and sexually. Yet a very large number of men, and perhaps all, are inclined toward treating women as inferior. Even in "enlightened" circles, lip-service paid to the equality of women with men is oftentimes undermined by the blindness of many men and frequently women too. This is a wounding blindness affecting both sexes. All of us, me included, need to be free of it.

How do we find healing? In speaking of the racist wound, Berry tells us he wants to know what the wound is, and how much he is suffering from it. Will this medicine cure us? Or do we need something else? If Berry is correct in his assessment of the racist wound, merely knowing what the wound is and how much he is suffering from it will not provide the cure, even though it will help. However, gaining such knowledge is a place to begin, and my goal is to make a start. It is not the only place to begin, but it is one place.

Berry speaks of the wound of White racism against Blacks. However, he extends his discussion in places to other White racisms and, in a brief sentence, to the oppression of women.[3] I shamelessly borrow from

---

2. I thank Susan J. McLeod-Harrison, Kendra Waddle Irons, Debbie Berho, Tom Johnson, and Phil Smith for comments on earlier drafts of this chapter.

3. Berry, *Hidden Wound*, 113.

Berry's rich and incarnate thought and thereby explore in more than a sentence the oppression of women and the wound my sexism creates in me. Although Berry's argument is a starting point, the true genesis of this essay is Susan McLeod-Harrison's comparison of racism and sexism and the rich conversations she and I have shared about the nature of sexism and patriarchy.[4]

Berry's understanding of racism is at once deeply personal and broadly cultural. First comes the story of his family who once owned slaves in Kentucky and second his analysis of the language that grew up around slavery and later around Black/White relationships in the South. Berry's writing exemplifies what Philip Hallie recognized as an ethic with a name attached.[5] If anyone is going to talk of living well, then she must be willing to move from the abstract to the personal and she must attach her name to any ethical proclamation. Berry masters both living well and standing by his words. His name is attached to his ethical positions, as is his life.

I've been a feminist since I was in college. For the last part of my college tenure, I attended two evangelical Christian liberal arts colleges and there found encouragement (from some quarters) to think about the equality of women and men. So began my long journey into discovering how deep the wound was in me. Before I left for college I was raised in a family typical of White, middle-class Canadians in Ontario. My grandparents are all, to my imperfect knowledge, of British/Scots descent. The imperfection—as I was taught mostly through whispers—was my paternal grandfather who was, as my father said, "no good." That meant something beside the fact that he may not have been of British/Scots descent.

I know little more. My father's mother never married and even after my father died, she refused to tell us my paternal grandfather's name. I had heard various accounts of my paternal grandfather, the most central of which was that he "got your grandmother drunk at a party." She was left with the baby.

I believe, but have no way of proving, that my father's birth was the result of rape or what we now call date-rape, as if the latter were any

---

4. Susan McLeod-Harrison has noted this comparison in our ongoing dialogue about feminism. For some work toward healing sexist wounds created by the Church, see McLeod-Harrison, *Saving Women from the Church*.

5. See Hallie, "From Cruelty to Goodness," 4–15.

less a rape for the apparently "polite" context and the apparently more "gentle" term attached to it. One consequence of history is that my paternal grandmother's relationship to our family, including my father, was rather rocky. She was, at the end of her long life, still on better terms with her neighbors and nurses than she was with her progeny. Although we visited her and helped her, she treated us as an embarrassment rather than as a family.

Berry begins his account of the wound of racism by writing the stories handed down on both sides of his family. Both families were slave owners. It is important, he says, to say how the stories came down to him. First, they were not forgotten and second, they were told casually. He writes, "The moral strain in them never reached me until some years after I had become a man."[6] Stories were told in my family as well. What interests me is not that the stories of deep hurt between the sexes were remembered and told casually but that they were remembered and not told at all. My father's history led to a large gap in my family's story telling.

I grew up in a close family, considering that my father worked a full-time job and ran a business too. My mother worked in the family business, as did all of us children as we grew. But we always ate dinner together and we always attended church together on Sundays. My maternal grandparents lived close by and we saw them often. My life was shaped by stories which both my father and mother told. My father's stories were different, for his began more or less when he joined the Canadian Air Force at seventeen. Little was mentioned of my father's family and my grandfather was never mentioned. None of us children connected with the fact that my grandmother's last name was identical to her mother's last name until much later. How could that be? As shocking as it was to think about this, we children one by one realized that Grandma—our Grandma—was never married. Let me hasten to add: I don't believe our shock was so much that she hadn't been married but that we were never told. Here the wound is opened in my history, for the evils and harms done in the name of sexism are so close to us we don't even speak of them.

My father's salvation, in some measure, was his being raised for the most part by his grandmother. From her my father learned to be the good man he was. No men lived in the house as my father grew, his own grandfather having died before he was born, his mother not being married and

---

6. Berry, *Hidden Wound*, 6.

only one of his aunts getting married later on. The all female household helped my father, I believe, learn to treat women if not as equals (this was the 30s and 40s in conservative Western Canada) at least as being due respect. My father was not above helping with housework when I was a child and although there were things my father did around the house that were typically "male," he did not reserve his efforts to only those.

Both my parents were raised in environments where work on the farm and the ranch was shared equally among the sexes, as was, to a lesser degree, the work in the house. I saw this carry over into my childhood as my father helped with the housework and as my mother, who during the day was a pretty "typical" stay-at-home 1950s mom, worked side-by-side in the evenings with my father in their business, which included janitorial work and rural postal delivery.

But I was raised to think and live with a sexist understanding of the world. My father, for all his respect for women, was not a feminist. He thought women more emotional than men (in general, at least) and this shaded his actions toward women. Although he admired women in public office (such as Margaret Thatcher) and he hired both women and men for all sorts of jobs, not just cleaning, he was still a man of his time and age. Women were referred to as "girls" and he didn't treat my sister the same as the boys in the family. The boys had much more freedom than did she. That was "normal" for the day.

Certainly my male friends all viewed women as somehow not only different from but inferior to men. We were all "girl watchers" as the 1960s pop song singer described himself. We all fantasized about sex and how to have as much sex short of intercourse as we could. We were, after all, good Christians. We all treated "girls" with the same ignorance and blindness as our fathers typically had. How exactly was I to know any different? Sexism was in the air I breathed, the work I did, the play I engaged in, and the dates I went on. Although longing for love and a good relationship, I never dated anyone longer than perhaps ten or twelve weeks—most often much shorter than that—and then broke it off. I dated a lot. With one or two exceptions, I did the breaking off. When a young woman once broke off our brief relationship I was affronted. How dare she?

When I was finally in a long-term relationship, I wrote to my then fiancée (and now late wife) "what do you plan to do as the wife of a Christian worker?" Her reply was scathing. I deserved her critical words, which included "what do you plan to do as the husband of a Christian worker?" I had no framework for thinking of the woman I was going to marry as anything other than my wife first and whatever else second. Thus began the long journey toward my feminist way of being in the world. I was twenty years old.

Since then I have tried to listen to women. I have tried to be egalitarian in how I interact with women. I have tried, in short, to be friends with women. In fact, in the thirty years or so since I began to think about the equality of women and men, I have tried to think, feel, and experience the world as a woman might.

I've been more or less an abysmal failure at the task. It took me a long time to discover, for example, that women (no more than men) do not all think, feel, or experience alike (a sexist assumption in itself), and to think they do is grossly to oversimplify the facts. Susan, my wife of four years, pointed out to me psychological data showing that men and women have far more in common than they have in difference. This still doesn't help me think, feel and experience as a woman. For I also see that what differences there are between women and men are embedded in a complex of cultural and historical circumstance. This makes sorting out what a particular woman thinks, feels or experiences as distinct from my experience as our cultural and historical circumstances. I can't experience the world as a woman for I am not a woman, and I can't experience the world as a particular woman for I am not that particular woman.

But I can sometimes come close. I've learned to listen for the words of men (and women) that characterize women in subtle but powerful ways as inferior to men. I'm learning to listen for power language and assumptions that men often use with men and that, when brought into discussions with women, are out of place. Why are they acceptable in one place and not the other?

In the late 1980s I taught an introduction to philosophy class whose focus for the day was sexism. I randomly picked a woman in the front row and asked her if she was a girl. She said yes. I asked her again. Again came the reply, yes. I asked her a third and a fourth and fifth time, each time trying to get her to feel the negative power of the language. At last she sat up in her chair, straightened up her body, threw her head and shoulders back in confidence and nearly shouted, "No, I'm a woman!" Her face lit up with understanding and clarity. I helped raise this young woman's consciousness. It was, I believe, one of the finest moments in all my teaching. But I wonder, had I used power inappropriately? Had I in fact pressured this young woman into a place she wasn't ready to go? I pray not, but I'll never know.

One year in the middle 1990s I took my then six-year-old son to a home-school gathering with other children twice weekly. Other than the man who came to lead the sports (who left immediately after his job was done), I was the only adult male present. For weeks and weeks I came together with the others when the request was made, "will all the moms gather over here please?" I sat with the moms and worked with the moms and talked with the moms for nearly a year before things changed. At first I was an outsider, and then I was the "guy" who could help move heavy objects, but finally I was included in conversations about child rearing and grocery shopping. But I was really given my "due" when the requests became "will all the moms and Mark gather over here, please?" This was a good experience for me. It helped me understand how a woman might feel when she is the only woman in a group of men. I had mixed feelings when I heard my inclusion with the moms get lost with my name.

I continue to struggle to understand. Recently I was talking to a new class about my now sixteen-year-old son and how sad it is that he is now taller than I am. I added, as a joke, that I was glad I could still beat him up. It was only afterward when I thought, "I don't believe that, and all that talk is about power and one-up-man-ship." My everyday speech does not always reflect what I want. A while ago, in my desire to force men not to be sexist, I far overstated my case in how men who are sexist should be treated in an academic context. The key word here is "force" — a power term my use of which points toward my lack of understanding, or worse, hypocrisy. I have far to go in understanding the wound that is in me and the consequences of the depth of that wound.[7]

The casualness with which Berry's family told its stories of slavery hid the moral strain in them. Years and a lot of effort led to him realizing that "in owning slaves, my ancestors assumed limitations and implicated themselves in troubles that have lived on to afflict me."[8] So too with me. My family and my friends, in being sexist, also assumed limitations and implicated themselves in troubles that have lived on to afflict me. They are limitations and troubles hard to see and harder still to overcome. The

---

7. Here I'd like to thank Corey Beals for helping me see that my pacifism isn't what it should be.

8. Berry, *Hidden Wound*, 6.

difference between my circumstance and Berry's is that the racism he inherited was specific to the United States and in particular to his ancestral ownership of slaves. The sexism I inherited was more universal. Only two Black families lived in my small Ontario town when I grew up and any racism aimed at them was not shared by virtually the whole culture. Women, in contrast, are everywhere present and men are everywhere sexist. (Plenty of racism existed then and does now in Ontario—First Nation peoples have borne perhaps the brunt of it in my home town, and perhaps the waves of Pakistani immigrants who moved in while I was in high school.)

Berry distinguishes between the private language of family memory and the public language of some of the hagiography by which Southern writers remember the "heroes" of the Civil War. The former "has conveyed what we know to have been true of ourselves but have not admitted or judged" and the latter conveys "what we *wish* had been true [italics his]."[9] What is our private language of family memory? For me, it includes the sealing over of a story of violence, of rape, of sexism at its worst. My own male ancestor, so far as I can tell, raped my grandmother. And if he didn't rape her, if she were a willing participant in the act that led to my father's birth, then my grandfather was at least an irresponsible man who did not care for his own child—he was, as my father said, no good. This is part of the silence of the private language of my family. Unlike in Berry's story, the public language too was silent on this matter. But the silence there was intended to let people think we had a "good" family. And we did, for the silence covered the pain and humiliation felt by my grandmother and my father.

The silence hid the history of sexism and the damage it had done both to my grandmother and my father and eventually to me. Opening the wound of the past, I am sure, would have brought further judgment on both my grandmother and my father. We lived in a sexist society and the hurts of raped women and their offspring are as plain as the language we all use to describe people with whom we don't get along. My dad would have been a bastard and my grandmother a bitch. After all, women who are raped deserve it, don't they? And their children are worthless, for they are not proper heirs to a name.

Berry writes (in the first person) that by telling what he has of his family stories that he hopes to have suggested

9. Ibid., 14.

... some of the historical and psychological forces that shaped my native language. It was a language that clearly had developed in the presence of Negroes who once had been slaves and who now were servants. Moreover, it was a language developed in an area of small farms, where whites and Negroes worked and dealt together with some intimacy. Within the context of prejudice and segregation, the two races had to get along, and so there was an etiquette of speech that one learned from the cradle: one "respected the feelings" of Negroes, when in their presence one did not flaunt one's "superiority" or use the word *nigger,* one called elderly Negroes Aunt and Uncle, and so on. But more important, *within* the language there was a silence, an emptiness, of exactly the shape of the humanity of the black man; the language I spoke in my childhood and youth was in that way analogous to a mold in which a statue is to be cast. The options, then, were that one could, by a careful observance of the premises of the language, keep the hollow empty and thus avoid the pain of the recognition of the humanity of an oppressed people and of one's own guilt in their oppression; or one could, willing or not, be forced by the occasions of sympathy and insight to break out of those premises into a speech of another and more particular order, so that the hollow begins to fill with the substance of a life that one must recognize as human and demanding.[10]

Similarly there is a hollow in our language about women, a silence we do not even yet notice. Berry writes that as a child and young man, he didn't notice the silence, the moral dimension to how he was eased casually into the language of prejudice. Yet if Berry didn't notice the silence in the racial language of his childhood, we as yet don't notice the rather complete silence in much of our language about women. For example, we don't, in the company of women, use the word "bitch" unless we are out and out sexist. But men do under their breath and behind the backs of women. And just as some Blacks refer to each other and themselves as "niggers," so do some women refer to each other, and themselves, as "bitches." But I do not think the silence in sexist language can be easily discovered by us, either women or men, by growing into adulthood, for so much of what we mean by adulthood is shaped by holding onto to certain patterns—hard, cruel and I daresay evil patterns—from childhood.

"Hey girls, that ladder might not be safe."

"Girls, the library is over there."

10. Ibid., 19.

"What's going on with the girls tonight?"

Having read these lines, of whom did you think? Your young daughters? The next door neighbor's preteen adolescents? Or was it the forty-five year old women at work? Or your mother?

The word "girl" is a diminutive. Yet we (often both women and men) use it to refer to women. By now, nearly everyone in academe knows that sexist language is unacceptable. Yet it persists. I submit that the use of the term "girl" to refer to adult women is no less prejudicial and harmful than the use of the term "boy" to refer to an adult Black man. It is a means of controlling and keeping women "in their place." And while we don't think of it or even notice it, the power of the language, the silence of the language, is present everywhere. This silence creates with it a wound in both women and men. It is a wound from which I want to be cured.

I want to shift to speak of culture at large, but in particular I want to speak of the culture I know best, the largely White middle class suburban culture of the evangelical church, and more specifically, the culture of the largely White suburban evangelical Christian colleges. To quote again from Berry:

> And so when I was a child my inherited language, so protective of a crucial silence at its heart, was still very near to the spiritual crises of its origin.... The racist language, which is to say the racist mentality, was still intact around its silence. I remember being told that Jesus loved the little black boys and girls as well as the little white ones. I even remember a Baptist Sunday school leaflet showing a little black boy in a group of white children standing before the Savior, being suffered to come unto Him. But I remember no attempt to reconcile this alleged divine love of black children with the white people's notion that they were inferior. I suppose it was assumed that if Jesus loved them there was no need for white folks to trouble themselves.[11]

The power of Berry's argument is not lost if we do a few substitutions. Consider this: And so when I was a child my inherited language, so protective of a crucial silence at its heart, was still very near to the spiritual crises of its origin.... The sexist language, which is to say the sexist mentality, was still intact around its silence. I remember being told that Jesus loved the little girls as well as the little boys. I even remember a

---

11. Ibid., 20, 21.

Baptist Sunday school leaflet showing a little girl in a group of boys standing before the Savior, being suffered to come unto Him. But I remember no attempt to reconcile this alleged divine love of little girls with the sexist notion that girls were inferior to boys. I suppose it was assumed that if Jesus loved them there was no need for sexist boys (and men) to trouble themselves.

Perhaps sexism is nowhere more alive than it is in our churches. Even with all the excellent scholarship (done by scholars committed to the authority of the Bible) in which it has been shown that Jesus was a person committed to the liberation of all people (in Christ there is neither slave nor free, Jew nor Greek, male nor female), we still have many people who simply do not admit that women can and should be in leadership in the Church. Although there remains controversy about much of the Bible and its patriarchy, there are cogent ways of reading and interpreting it that not only allow for but encourage the view that Jesus came to set us all free from the power structures that oppress and bind us.

While I wish it were a surprise to me, the sexism in evangelical Christian colleges is not. Nearly every term I ask my students at George Fox University, the evangelical Christian university where I teach, whether or not women are equal to men. The resounding reply is yes, of course. But when I ask if women can be pastors, many, many demur, both women and men, from saying yes. Perhaps they too think that if Jesus loves the women as well as the men, then there is no need for the Church to bother itself about the matter.

Taking the risk of a generalization drawn only from my own observations, I suggest that the apparent conflict in my students is one most professors at evangelical colleges feel too. Most of us encourage both women and men into the professions—medicine, research, teaching, and so forth—but typically not into the ministry per se. Why is this, and why the bifurcation? Perhaps we have not done our exegetical homework or perhaps our hermeneutical circles don't quite overlap with Paul's proclamation that in Christ there is no male or female. These are speculations. But what is not a speculation is the number of women students who come to my feminist colleagues and me, sometimes in anger but often in great sadness. These are students who feel the need to leave the Church because they feel they have no home there. I wonder how they can have no home with Jesus. Could it be that they simply don't see Jesus in the Church?

When will the subtleties of sexism end? How can I be cured? I can only take one step at a time and a first step is to acknowledge, again, that the parallel I am drawing between racism and sexism belongs to Susan McLeod-Harrison. She has repeatedly said that if we talked about Blacks the way we talk about women, we would be accused—and rightly so—of deep prejudice. For example, if I say women are less rational then men, we don't blink an eye, or perhaps we wink an eye. If I were to say Blacks are less rational than Whites, I would lose my job. Susan is right and I am a better person for her insight. The more general point here is that men need to listen to women. Really listen. I've been trying to listen for thirty-one years. I've learned more in the last three or four years than in the first twenty-seven or so. I am a slow learner. But I'm now angrier and sadder and I see further and feel deeper. When we listen, our capacity to hear, really hear, increases exponentially. If the wound is really hidden, and if the silence is really deeper than that surrounding racism, we must listen carefully with renewed ears to what women are saying. Or sometimes what they are not saying. Or don't feel free to say. Or won't say in the presence of men, unless the men are "safe." Racism itself is a problem so deep it is hard to see how to resolve it. Sexism is deeper yet.

A second step is to help bring about consciousness-raising for both women and men. Not all women are aware of the subtleties of sexism and consequently it takes time and love to help a woman come to realize that the way she is treated, and even the way she thinks of herself, is because men and many women have bought into the patriarchy of our homes, churches, communities and societies.

A third move is to avoid the notion that what women want is male guilt. I taught a feminist philosophy class some years ago and came home daily feeling beaten up by the readings. Men were often, but not always, cast as a major source of evil—and not wrongly so. My guilt nearly froze me, and my response for a while was to think that I could not find a solution so there was no point in trying. Guilt is not a great motivator in finding positive solutions. Dialogue and listening are.

A fourth stride is recognizing that men already have privileged positions and if we become feminists, then we can speak out against sexism. I must caution myself, however, not always to presume that I understand the mind of the women for whom I am speaking out. But the sad logic of the situation is that sexism is so subtle that if a woman makes a point in favor of women, she is often cast as a trouble-maker whereas if the same point is made by a man, he is only speaking the truth. The fact of the matter is, women who speak out are often cast as "bitches" and their voices, no matter how much truth they may carry, are simply not heard.

A fifth measure is not to cry foul when a feminist woman or man points out some way in which we men are sexist, whether it is a general observation or aimed more personally. Is it the language we use, the practices we keep, or the way we subtly treat women differently than men? When someone notes it, instead of becoming defensive or hurt—or at least instead of staying defensive and hurt—be noble enough to do some soul searching to find out why the criticism was suggested in the first place. Even if the criticism comes out of someone's anger, I think most of that anger is righteous and a lot of it comes out of the harm done by sexism in the first place.

A final step in this woefully inadequate list is to persist in uncovering the wound and its consequences, to recognize when our language and actions undermine the value of women as people, and to continue to learn how our patriarchal attitudes and culture shape us. For example, Susan and I talk regularly about our eighteen-month old son and wonder how to help him grow into a man who takes for granted not only in his head but in his heart that women and men are equal. The conversation is an on-going one, since the issue is deeply complex. How much is nature, how much nurture, how much is personal, and how much cultural? We do not know all the answers. Nor can we find them alone. But there is hope, I believe. As we learn how to nurture our little girls and boys with equality, with good role models and equal support from both mothers and fathers, we can begin to shift the ground.

Sexism is deeply rooted in human being—part of the fall of humanity from God's intention for us. But bemoaning the fact and simply continuing to live in the sin that shapes so much of our society and culture, so much of our church life and, indeed, our lives themselves, are not enough. We need to stand against the patriarchy and the misuse of power that is endemic to our lives. We need to stand together as women and men, as followers of the Incarnate Word who dwells among us, as those who hope some day to be fit to be invited into the inner circle of equality that is the Trinity in whom we believe. We need to stand together against the damaging and damning sin that is sexism.

Sexism. I want to be cured, and I do not want to pass it on to my children.

20

Community

In "A Quiet Chamber Kept for Thee,"[1] Walter Wangerin Jr. tells a wonderful story about hope and fear. It is a story about a cold, cold Christmas Eve in Edmonton in 1954, the year he had become an adult, the year he gave up hope.

The story's cold passed into my bones the first time I read it. Perhaps it drilled its way into my sinews because I hadn't known before that Wangerin is Canadian, at least by upbringing. I'm Canadian too, and still awandering down here in the "States" as my relatives all call the U.S.—a fact observed and puzzled over by my American-born and raised oldest son when he was eight as we returned home to San Antonio after visiting my side of his extended family over Christmas 1998. As well, at Christmas-time 1954 I hadn't yet been born. That event still harbored over thirteen months away. But I remember some of the things Wangerin remembers. Milk being delivered to the door, wanting the cold to come so we would know it was Christmas, the slow buildup of excitement amongst my two brothers, my sister and me.

But perhaps most of all I remember, as Wangerin does, becoming adult. It happened to me when I was a little older than was Wangerin (perhaps I was a slower learner) but happen it did. He writes, "I've implied that we were all excited on that particular Christmas Eve morning, and so we were; but though my brothers and sisters could manifest their excitement with unbridled delight, I could not mine. I absolutely refused

---

1. Wangerin, "Quiet Chamber."

to acknowledge or signal excitement. They loved the sweet contractions in their stomachs. I was afraid of them. For I had that very year become an adult: silent, solemn, watchful, and infinitely cautious."[2] When I read those words, I knew that Wangerin had crept into my dreams one night and snatched those feelings away from me, that somehow, a man I'd never met and I were brothers.

I, too, became an adult. I, too, gave up on hope. Just as Wangerin, so went I. When I became an adult, I realized that to hope is to be a fool; to hope is to be deceived; to hope is to die, as Ben Franklin put it, "fasting." And just as Wangerin writes, "I held myself in a severe restraint. Because—what if you hope, and it doesn't happen? It's treacherous to hope. The harder you hope, the more vulnerable you become. And what if you believe a thing, but it isn't true? Well, the instant you see the deception, you die a little."[3]

And I had died, a little. It was the Christmas when the lights came on and no magic was under the tree, the Christmas the presents were just as real, but not as big as I had imagined, the Christmas I hoped there would be peace on earth, but wars still raged.

Wangerin's story is about how his hope returned, grace was made manifest, and his heart was turned from stone to fire. It's about how a child's heart was melted by his father's love, grace, and understanding. The second time I read the story, seven years had passed. But I was drawn to it by memory the night of the second reading, for the week of the second reading I lost my hope, again. I ran it screaming out of my life with as much violence as I could muster, and I was afraid I couldn't find it. I chased it out with a large knife, cutting and lancing away at the boils of my life.

As a professional philosopher, I know all about the problem of evil. I know exactly how difficult the evil stain of sin is to remove. But life is more brutal than even I had imagined. The rooms of the philosopher still have stained glass. It's only when the glass is broken that one sees the brutal reality of broken, ravaged people, and smells the stench of rotted pus. But I've been a skeptic nearly all my life. Indeed, it's exceeding difficult to tell whether I became a professional philosopher because I was a skeptic or a skeptic because I was a philosopher. I've been like the people who told Jesus during the triumphal entry to keep his disciples,

2. Ibid., 59.
3. Ibid., 59.

who were calling out his praises, quiet. But I've also known that if the disciples were to hold their peace, the very stones would cry out. Hope was never dead in me.

Until the week to which I've referred, the week of lost hope. What happened was, in some sense, a mere straw of a thing. After all, one of my best high school friends had muscular dystrophy, his brother had polio, his sister needed numerous, serious back surgeries, and his mother—my "second mom"—died in horrible pain with multiple sclerosis. I'd seen plenty of suffering. My late wife who had a very promising career to begin with a nearly minted PhD from Yale came down with Lupus—a chronic, auto-immune disease wherein the body attacks itself—and lived a life truncated by monstrous pain, surgeries, and doctor's visits. I wondered if she wouldn't become like my high school friend and simply stop seeing the doctors who, as Piers Ploughman says "are mostly murderers, God help them!—their medicines kill thousands before their time."[4] Although she had some terrific MDs, she also was a magnet for bad ones. It is of note that the word "chronic" is traceable back to the Greek god Kronos who ate his own children but who mistook a rock for Zeus, who eventually took revenge on Kronos. And it's related to the word "chronicle," a story of a life lived, or time passed through. Except that my late wife was doing time rather than living in it.

So suffering is not a stranger to me. It is an old companion. Yet with the week of lost hope came the straw. But straws, when driven by tornadoes, can be driven straight into the heart of a tree. The straw was this. Our family attended a weekly meeting of Christians to worship, pray and support one another. Several people we had known for two or three years, others only a year. The pastors of the church were a couple my late wife and I had known well in college, twenty years before.

I long ago learned that those of us who hold PhDs can make people nervous, so in church settings, I'd leave my questions behind. I was there to support, not challenge. For nine months or longer I had sat through weekly "talks" by the leader of the group, talks I often found problematic. Yet I kept my questions to myself. One night, the leader waxed on about how God heals people when they have faith. After the talk was over and most people had left, I simply stated that God hadn't healed my (now late) wife (who was still alive) when we had prayed fervently for her. I

---

4. Langland, *Piers Ploughman*, 194.

was really just asking for some moral support. The leader told me that I was beyond him. He didn't know how to help.

Within the week, we were asked to leave the gathering. We were asked to leave because the leader thought I had challenged his authority. When I asked whether the pastor knew about this, I was told that the group's leader had the pastor's blessing and authority to remove us. Anger is not the word to describe my reaction. Rage is closer. I raged at God. I raged at the group leadership. I raged at the pastor "friend" who blessed the leadership. A final, crushing blow, from a straw.

At the heart, however, was the gospel. Where was the process? Where were the questions of us? Where were the years of trust built up through common work and commitment? Gone, washed away by insecurity and false judgment. For all the suffering, physical, emotional, and spiritual we had been through, why was this so painful? It was, I think, a breech of the sacramental relationship among friends, like a priest spitting into the communion chalice just before it is held to the communicant's lips. I could stand it no longer. Hope disappeared, the gospel sat in wrecks along the side of the road I'd traveled. I left the house and drove and drove, and raged and raged. I came to my office. It was in a modern academic building with beige walls and a view overlooking the courtyard of the university. But it wasn't a warm office; it didn't bespeak of home and friends and family. It was simply a place to go so I would not take out my frustration on my innocent family.

Along one wall was my desk and computer table—all the accoutrements of a professor's office. Along the opposite wall were the bookshelves. As I sat, thinking, crying, despairing, I heard my Canadian brother calling to me from the books. I simply remembered Wangerin's story, turned my chair, reached for the book, opened up to the essay and read.

Augustine says this of memory and God: "But where within my memory do you abide, Lord, where do you abide? What kind of abode have you fashioned for yourself? What manner of sanctuary have you built for yourself? So great an honor have you given to my memory as to abide within it!" He continues, after showing that God is not in the chambers of the senses nor is he identical to the mind itself: "Where then did I find you, so that I might learn to know you?" And then, "Too late have I loved you, O Beauty so ancient and so new, too late have I loved you! Behold, you were within me, while I was outside: it was there that I sought you, and a deformed creature, rushed headlong upon these things of beauty which you have made. You were with me, but I was not with you."[5]

It was in memory that hope returned. God, hidden among the debris of suffering and pain strewn among the memories of my life, spoke out to me. The divine nudged me toward hope, nudged me toward my brother, Wangerin, who himself had lost hope. I was beside myself—St. Augustine says "you were within me, while I was outside." I was beside myself, I'd lost my mind, I'd come undone, for hope had died.

Hope had died for I had forgotten; I had forgotten the wonder of the communion of saints. I had forgotten the wonder that my family still loved me. I had forgotten that Jesus on the cross was all alone, yet there were two, John the Beloved and Mother Mary. Did Jesus hope on the cross? As Mary, who kept all these things and pondered them in her heart, and John, who had seen Jesus transfigured, stood at the foot of the cross, Jesus called them together in the communion of saints and says, "son, behold your mother; mother, behold your son." Jesus hoped for the future as he hung dying.

The straw wasn't so big, but it was symbolic of eight years of misery, cut off from community, cut off from real fellowship, as we lived the life of Job, exiled away from nearly all we loved. Job's story, too, is in my memory, and although Job receives back his riches and stature, he doesn't get his original children back. As hope was passed through the fires of refinement, Job's perspective changed.

So has mine. Oh, we worked it out. We met later with the pastor and the leader and we were allowed back into the group. But it wasn't the same. Neither was I. I learned, again, that one must trust people, but not be surprised when they disappoint you. And hope returned, just as it always does, through memory, and Christ, and the communion of saints, that great "democracy of the dead." I heard not only Christ, but Job, John, Mary, Augustine and Walter Wangerin. I had heard them calling me, renewing hope and hoping for renewal. Hope will kill you, it's true. But hope also redeems, a mystery in which we all need to dwell. Brutal hope, redeeming hope. Hope, memory, and community.

---

5. Augustine *Confessions* 10.38.

21

Time

I sit today in my office, as the cold weather finally comes to Oregon. My new colleague tells me it never stays hot after the middle of September. September died and October was born before his prediction about the cold and rain came through, late but better. After eight years in the suffering heat of Texas, the cool weather doesn't come too early for my taste. The north creeps down to make the days shorter and darker. The north is good. Real seasons are important to me. Fall and winter in Texas simply run together, and winter seems never fully able to make itself stick. When exiled in Texas, I missed the snow on the trees and the possibility of snow castles. Even though we don't get much of that in Oregon either, at least it is considerably below 75 degrees.

In my office, I sit amidst the books piled high on my desk; the work of ten lifetimes, even should I put my mind to it. I sit amidst the thoughts of Plato and Rousseau, of Kant, and all their friends, so enlightened, so knowing. I wonder if they ever thought the cold would never come? I wonder, too, if they ever thought the world too unkind, too cruel to offer even half a cup of cold water to some slobbering idiot along the road. How corrupt, how terrible a world of theory, not knowing the cold in one's bones, nor the love of an outstretched hand.

No Plato am I, no Rousseau, no Kant. Many days, I'm not even a friend. Of what value are my thoughts of high and lofty things, of Plato's forms, of angels so tiny that thousands can dance on the head of a pin? The work overwhelms me. I write no more not because I'm out of ideas or even out of ink. The leaves of the fall trees hang on, but they know they're doomed. Like the leaves, I too am doomed. I'm out of hope. No lover of wisdom I, for lovers have hope.

Cups of water aren't my strength either. No saint am I. No Joan of Arc, no Teresa of Avila, no John of the Cross. I am the man among the tombs, *before* he was touched by Jesus and made a saint, slightly atilt the world. I'm a thief with someone else's ideas. I steal and repeat them, dressing them up for my students. I have no lofty thoughts, nor have I good thoughts. I have thoughts of the dark. The north comes down with darkened, shortened days.

It is cold outside. Fall has come and winter? It's around the corner, colder yet, and darker. But in the winter, in the dark of the cold north country from whence sprung my life, Christmas happens. Of course it's all covered over with songs and tinsels so shiny they'd make an angel blush. Still it happens. No matter how dark my life, no matter how cloudy the sky, hope returns to me each Christmas. For Christmas is a true gathering, the Great Thanksgiving of Christ, in which the communion of all the saints meets.

At Christmas, God saw the dark. At Christmas, God knew the suffering of being born: God the Fetus, God the Embryo, and God the Holy Zygote. This is the God I worship, this is the God I know: the God who saw the dark inside of Mary's womb, the God of the Dark. How can God have seen these things? How can God's head and shoulders have cramped small enough to pass through Mary's vagina? In truth God passes through. In our stead God passes through. In darkness God passes through. It is a cramping that leads to death, a bloody death. And darkness again, the darkness of the stone-cold grave, the darkness of sickness, the darkness of our empty human lives. So with winter comes the dark, and with the winter comes the God of the Dark.

Winter also brings the light. For God is not just God the Fetus, God the Embryo, and God the Holy Zygote. The divine is also God the Maker, God the Lover, and God the Holy Wooer. This is also the God I worship. And so hope begins. I think those thoughts of lofty heights, of Plato's forms, of angels dancing. For my thoughts are redeemed, again and again and again. They are thoughts of tomorrow, of better days, of cold water that's free to all, of spouses no longer ill, of parents no longer dying, of children no longer hurt by angry words or angry hands, of peace on earth, good will toward all. The God of the Dark is also the

God of the Light, and God of the Hope—my hope and my joy and my patience to endure the suffering of the dark, of being human, of being born, of living history.

Several weeks have passed. Today is the last Sunday of "ordinary time," the time in the Church year between Pentecost and Advent. This week's lectionary readings are mostly about the end time, times of glory, times of gore and judgment. So it seems ordinary time is not so ordinary. During ordinary time judgment comes to wreak its havoc, to disrupt our lives, to end our work-a-day world. If ordinary time leads up to judgment, what is to be said? Again next week we start anew; the season of waiting takes over, as we look toward the Advent of our Lord and Savior. Advent leads to Christmas, Christmas to the Feast of Innocents. What a day, the Feast of Innocents! As fear and anger and sheer meanness take over Herod's life, the children of Bethlehem are slaughtered, one by one, as cruel soldiers walk through the village, slicing throats like so much bread.

Jesus escapes through a dream, but only for a while. He, too, will finally fall under the blade, the water and blood gushing forth. The Feast of Innocents is not lost to Jesus. His innocence is lived out for thirty odd years and then killed under the hands of the soldiers. One imagines a young soldier assigned the dirty work of Herod at the cribs of babes, later standing, like the Roman centurion, at the foot of the cross, in the dark, sighing "surely this was the Son of God." In the intervening years, how many innocent people had he run through? On Good Friday, this soldier, standing in the dark at the foot of the cross, perhaps realizes he has always been in the dark. Is he now able to see the light? O, blessed innocents, O blessed knife that killed for Jesus' sake! How can our God know the light and yet live in the dark? The throats sliced on the day of the Innocents are truly like so much bread, the body of our Lord, offered in our pain, and suffering, and agony. Jesus shared in their pain, suffering and agony. They did not die alone. Yet what a price for them to pay, so Jesus could slip away into the night, and escape death for a while. Can this evil be redeemed? Can God so operate as to redeem and transform this ugliness into something beautiful? I do not understand. Yet I believe.

So with Innocents over, we look toward Epiphany, the day Mary and Joseph are visited by the Magi. Epiphany is the day on which the star gazers come to bow down to One foretold by the alignment of planets, or a bright shining star, or something unusual in the Western sky. The Shepherds had already bent their knees before the manger. One suspects by now that Mary, Joseph, and Jesus have found better shelter than the straw-matted stable. Yet how good could the shelter be? They are not wealthy, and this trip of theirs is no vacation. No matter how good the shelter, it is surely not the streets of gold to which Jesus is accustomed. Into this shelter come the Magi, singing the praises of the One who made the universe, God Incarnate, the Holy Word, dwelling among us. They look back to the day when Jesus was born. How odd it must seem to them, that this King for whom they have sacrificed to come these hundreds of miles, was born amidst the sheep and chickens. Yet they, too, just as the shepherds before them, bend their knees.

Did they look back in wonder at the day of Jesus' incarnation? How should we look back, I wonder? Christmas, the Mass of Christ, is the day we celebrate Jesus' birth. The day of this Holy Eucharist, the day of this Great Thanksgiving, is a day unlike all others. For as the presence of Christ is with us on this day, in the breaking of bread, in the drinking of wine, we recall not just his death, but his birth, the birth of God among us. It was a birth unlike all others, a birth in which the darkness of the human soul is captured by the light of the heart of God's divine being. No great ideas, no thought of any human alone, can match the thought of God dipping into history, taking on a human self, projecting the divine being toward ordinary time. For Jesus doesn't just participate with us in Advent or Lent or Holy Week and Easter. He participates in ordinary time too. He is in our work, for he worked, he is in our leisure, for he leisured, he is in our laughter, for he laughed, and he is in our sorrow, for he sorrowed. He knows us from the inside out. How else could God show the divine love for us? To redeem the dark, God must know the dark. And so it was that Mary Magdalene does not remain estranged from God. She is redeemed and made atilt the world. She is transformed by Christ, the living incarnate Word, the one who in birth took on our very natures so that in death, he could kill death, and in resurrection, he could enable us to survive death and destruction and the natural corruption of our bodies. Jesus redeems us by going into the pit and paying the price to set us free from slavery to the evil one. He takes the dark and transforms it into light, just by being there among us. In the incarnation, God provides for the human person the ability to survive corruption, redeeming our thoughts, our work, our being. Ordinary time is transformed into extraordinary time. This is the power that lives in the dark to redeem it, swallowing up darkness, suffering, and evil of all sorts. This is the power of the Lord.

May ordinary time come to an end, may Christ come in judgment. May we be redeemed in him through Easter faith and hope. Come Lord Jesus! Come Lord Jesus, be our guest, and all these things to us please bless. Amen.

Appendix

Words and the World

Sky hooks. Left-handed monkey wrenches. Buckets of steam. Each is a bane of new apprentices in factories and workshops. Sent once for a box of sky hooks at eleven or twelve years of age, I was the brunt of laughter for several days. I did not learn the lesson. Years later, as a member of a group newly apprenticed to the master mechanics of philosophy, I was sent looking to acquire sky hooks again. The question was set before us novices, motivated by Platonic dreams. The inquiry, we were solemnly told, stood alone among all philosophical questions as axial, the life-blood. How do words hook onto the world?

Not sensing the contour of the ground as similar to my earlier trip to the hardware store, I, and all the rest of us, went looking for the hooks. We tried desperately to understand the connections we needed to make, with little succor from our masters, and little laughter too, whether at us or with us. Seeking sky hooks can be a lonely business. Such abstract, lonely seeking generates no more success than discovering how to love someone by reading medical textbooks about sex. Theoretical approaches lack embodiment, flowers without fruit. Although the question was raised as the only philosophical question worth asking, and although the question was repeated—often, in studies from Plato to Frege—we were also taught the question by what was left unsaid and undone. The irony did not journey unnoticed.

The question was not the question of suicide. I remember one professor scoffing at Camus's silliness in placing the question of suicide at the center of philosophy. I did not know then that my-now-late-wife would manage to write a few very important words the hour or so before the painkillers took her.

The question was not the question of how to live, either. Only the meaning of "life," not the meaning of life: thus went a response to W. V. O. Quine in a Harvard alumni magazine printed about the time of his retirement. Clever, and directly to the point, Quine's interviewer not only summarized the drift of Quine's philosophy but much analytic philosophy in general during the last century, and to an equal degree, much continental philosophy.

The question was not the question of how to be good. We can ask only concerning words about the good and not concerning words that are good. We can ask only the status of the words, per se, and about not the status of a person's worth. Persons seem just *persona*, masks and nothing more. Much contemporary philosophy acts with the belief that if we lose our masks, little is left. Our masks turn out thinner than the words we utter, and made of flimsier material too. Our masks lack even the breath to bring them into the world, whereas words can hang in the air, suspended in the wind. If the phonates are phony, the persons are only *personae*. The last century or so of philosophy hides behind masks and does not deal with persons, whenever it deals with words and not with worth. The emphasis on words, to the denigration of worth, is a kind of heresy as G. K. Chesterton used the word.

Do we just have words and nothing else? Do we just have word sand, what they grip (as if where the letters are placed makes no real difference, or perhaps the utter difference, to the way things are)? Do we just have words as power, eagle's talons swooping down from some heavenly (or hellish) place to rip flesh, torn from unsuspecting prey or, as in *The Name of the Rose*, bringing our dead bodies (on the hook) over a vat of pig's blood, to let our deaths drown in red, ruining the pudding? (I was once told by a professor not to use red ink to correct student papers as it "inflames the students." Shades of heresy hunting.) Will the words we use create the apocalypse written of so well in the ancient abbey's story, where libraries are labyrinths, laughter lugubrious, and logic a lure? *Ex libris* Aristotle, have we had created for us, an ex-library?

(Metaphors should not be taken too seriously, we philosophical neophytes were told, (unless you were Max Black or Heidegger). (And look where Heidegger ended up—in the Black Forest, reading poetry). (I do not think it was Max Black's Forest, unless, of course, you read philosophy like Stanley Cavell and the like (of course, Cavell did not like saying things like "and the like" because if the things are alike, one would not have to note them, and if they are not alike, then one should list them), and made Quine and Derrida first cousins). (Oh, we were speaking of metaphors and Heidegger. Perhaps we should talk about another professor who leaned over to a visiting speaker who had just lectured about metaphor. The first said to the second (to be precise), "You won't find many in this department (of philosophy) worried about metaphors. They don't know about them." Of course they had all read Max Black...) (But to get away from philosophy (can we ever?), what if you take things into your own hands, like the former assistant professor of English who (failing to get tenure) opened a bar near the university called "The English Department"). (It was a popular place, in a "masses" sort of way, but although wine was served there, it was not a church). (I'm sure he made more money as a bar keep than as one of us academic types (or are we tokens of the type?—a philosopher's distinction (a distinction run amuck or through the muck (at least))). (And did you hear the one about the philosopher whose sentences were like an infinite set of left-handed parentheses, spoken of the philosopher who said "you won't find many in this department worried about metaphors." His talk seemed one long metaphor, and hence, by the end of the semester, one wondered if anything had been said.) (Parentheses are sort of like hooks, but that is a simile, not a metaphor). Speaking of hooks (I have dropped enough names by now (one wonders how one drops a name. It is not like names can be carried around in a box, exactly. Our old standard philosophy joke was "how can a door be ajar," understood to be "how can a door be a jar," spoken with the proper British accent)): But speaking of names and hooks:

If not hooks,	,skooh ton fI
words mirror reality,	,ytilaer rorrim sdrow
reflecting it back,	,kcab ti gnitcelfer
or make it,	,ti ekam ro
or maybe they	(it's in the illustrations—the rooster,
hide it	maybe, who sometimes
in marginalia,	represents Jesus and sometimes the devil)
or in the bigness	SSENGIB eht ni ro
of our LITTLENESS,	ssenelttil ruo fo

> they hawk our
> goods in tomorrow's new universe
> next door.

> ruo kwah yeht
> esrevinu wen s'worromot ni sdoog
> .rood txen

In the twenty-first century, the words on this page are no thicker than the ink, or more ephemeral yet, electronic shots in the dark. Reality separate from words? Heresy. In the old days, a word disconnected from reality was called lying. What we call it now is radical postmodernism: words making realities in which no lie is possible. Can we still use logic? Although "lies" and "falsehoods" do not share all of the same Venn circle, one of the reasons there can be no lies in radical postmodernism is that there can be no falsehoods, and if there can be no falsehoods, there can be no truth either. But then, logic is undermined, or at least its usefulness in evidence. The whole basket of ideas seems to lose integrity, and once the basket loses integrity, no one can put eggs into it. What if someone does—put eggs into it, that is—what kind of world is created? Surely not a clean one.

Integrity includes the connecting of words and person into a whole; in measuring only words and not people, we have become a poorer race. I still believe our words can stand taller than the ink, and the weirdness of typing poems in cyberspace does not undo one's being. I still believe our words can reach further than paltry sales jobs about alternative universes. (I think e.e. cummings at least believed there was a universe to have an alternative to—it was the cheapening of words, the advertising of words that seemed to bother him. Nowadays it's not clear we even have a universe, the way some of us talk. Should we be listening?)

I still believe our words can, instead, make one a person who won't be bought, or sold, or mortgaged for a reality that does not exist. One is more than the words on this sheet of paper. Words do stand in one's stead, they do not merely stand on their head and neither does the world, *pace* William of Baskerville's disciple, one Adso of Melk, in *The Name of the Rose*. "In the beginning was the Word and the Word was with God, and the Word was God." So begins the Gospel of John and *The Name of the Rose*. John's Gospel, of course, expresses that Jesus is God, always has been, is, and will be. When God becomes Incarnate, God does not cease to be God. Yet this is not the only reading of the opening words of John. In *The Name of the Rose*, much less clarity attends the famous words, a hint of the ambiguity that follows in the novel. Instead of God being conceived of as the word, the word is conceived of as God. Or at least, so one can read the sentence.

Against that reading, and a major struggle in *The Name of the Rose* itself, is the question of how words relate to reality and reality to words. Certainly the Church has proclaimed that in the beginning was the Word and so began the world. The Church has proclaimed that such creativity is definitively not our task. Human words do not make the world *ex nihilo*, even if, as I believe, we can make alternative ontologies within the world). Instead, words make the world better. As Adso of Melk said: "Such is the power of truth that, like good, it is its own propagator."[1]

We should wonder if that's true. Or good. Or maybe, at least, beautiful. Perhaps we let Adso's observation pass simply because we think it *is* beautiful. These days, that is often enough. But do we not long for the days when the three were one, and the one, three. (I have to be careful not to wax nostalgic here. I would not want to be accused of heresy myself, and simply wish for some things from the past that were more fixed.) In the old days, at least we could count. Or perhaps count on something not changing simply because we gave it a different name. Should we count the way William of Baskerville did, or some other way? The unwinding of the universe seemed to begin with the other William, William of Ockham, and Roger Bacon. (The postscript tells us Eco thought of having William of Ockham as the detective in the story. Eco changed his mind when he found Ockham to be a less than attractive human—a connecting of word to being, an integrity needed for the story). Should it end with them? Perhaps they asked the wrong questions, even if they were right at the time, or at the right time, and who is to say, with all the ins and outs of medieval, modern, and post-modern in the novel? As to the heresy hunters, the inquisitors who contrast with William of Baskerville, and who almost win over Adso (he did, after all, end up writing down the story, in some fashion, even though he had become lost in God), their problem is not rooted in metaphysics. They are not ignorant of something important because of human limitations. Nor are they trying to reach something we can not. Those men are just evil. This judgment is easier to make about fictional characters, of course. Perhaps integrity requires it of the real item? We can not play semantics all the time without evil running wild, and if we reduce evil to semantics, do we not lose real evil amongst the words?

1. Eco, *Name of the Rose*, 25.

So although "evil" is a word we must be cautious of using, like the word "lie," it seems to pick out something that's missing. Perhaps Augustine's meontic theory of evil, wherein evil is like a hole (and also not a whole—but again, there is an importance to getting the right word) that depends for its (lack of real) being on the being of the good that surrounds it. A hole is no less real for being dependent.

Power can be used for evil. Power is not thereby evil. Authority can be used to force others to submit. But authority is not simply positional, it's earned. Someone might have "authority" because the person has power, but that kind of authority is not real, even for God. Such "authority" seems driven purely by greed attached to power. When we think words have power all on their own, without integrity, then the person wielding the power has no true authority, only force.

We disarm false authority when we do not seek it. We undo power when we seek humility. Words are themselves humble things. "Humility" is related to "humus." We walk over humus everyday. Words are nearly breathless things. But out of humus and breath we are made. Humility seeks words that do not falsify, that do not seek to create false power. When we grant authority to people to whom it does not belong because we let words have their way with us, we deny our own integrity. Our own words need a whole person giving them voice. When the voice is one of truth, we have integrity.

"Such is the power of truth that, like good, it is its own propagator." To propagate is to cause to multiply, to pass on from one generation to the other, to make a thing known. If we are to stand against true evil (I hate to mix those two words together—is there some way to admit the actual presence of evil without giving it a positive, ontological status?), then it seems we must also recognize evil, and if we recognize evil, do not we have to recognize good? If good is its own propagator, then good not only causes itself to multiply and to pass on from one generation to the next, but to make itself known. Plato's old puzzles about the Good linger, yet we do not need a Socratic definition to recognize good when we see it.

So with truth. Truth causes itself to multiply, and passes on generation to generation. Truth can be understood for what it, itself, is, namely, reality. Truth is the way things are, not just words about the way things are. Is there a single way things are? Maybe. Maybe not. In trying to find out, we keep running up against our own epistemologies and then confusing them for the way things are. None of which gets us around the metaphysical shudder mentioned in the postscript of *The Name of the Rose*. But even if things are several ways the world is, that is, even there are several realities as many these days are wont to admit, reality remains, the ontological mystery. The postmodern can not annihilate reality completely. Enough seems left over to share, and even if many realities exist, they are not completely separable or independent. Radical postmodernism, in its attempt to deny reality, leaves words alone. Words are thus real and that gives us a sort of reality. Reality is not easily escaped, and epistemology is not metaphysics, at least not without a lot of hard work. If we have a reality in words themselves, we can move to sorting other reality with words. Metaphysics looms large again. The task left undone for us is the sorting of various versions of reality, and therefore sorting which overarching version of reality, rightly renders our experience and the things contained within. God and philosophy peek again from behind the shuddering curtain pulled back briefly from across the sky.

To get around the shudder of the radically postmodern, we have to embrace the world and not simply words. In embracing the world, we embrace the Other and thereby name the social core of reality. That is integrity. Integrity is living the words we speak and write, not hiding behind the pages or even the ink. Integrity is facing the evils of the world and not ignoring the fact that I, too, am tainted, that I, too, am caught up in evil. Integrity includes moving from the speculations in which so many philosophers and theorists live and handing a cup of cold water to someone who is thirsty. Integrity is the placing (or is it a re-placing?) of words into the social realm in which they belong, as true communication among friends and neighbors. Integrity is a homecoming.

When I was a young teacher, a student reported one of the literature professors as announcing "language is ontological." I laughed out loud. Now older, and I hope wiser, I, too, see words as real. If they are not, I do not see how they hook onto the world. I have discovered that they hook pretty simply. They hook onto the world by my reaching out with my hands and not simply by opening my mouth. Human relationship is essential, as is connecting my words to my intentions and their concomitant actions. I simply have to do what I say I will do.

How do words, then, hook onto the world? Not with sky hooks. They hook onto the world by us using them well and properly, that is, by using them as a good. We can not just have words instead of the world.

We must have words in our stead in the world. Integrity links words and the world. We should look and see how things are, even while they may be shaped by out shared words, and not simply name things the way we want them to be, whether good or evil. An evil cannot be made good simply be renaming it, and neither can a good be made evil. Words hook onto the world by us using them to make the world better, because we cannot just make the world any way we wish. Feeling the metaphysical shudder, even making the shudder feel pleasurable, as *The Name of the Rose* is intended to do, does not free us from calling things the way they are. Our words are real and they make a difference, not in some divinely creative way but in a humanly creative way. Yet these are not, I deeply and lovingly believe, so far separate. Words are true when we follow through in making goodness and beauty. Words hook onto the world with our intention, with our goodness, and with our beauty. Words hook onto the world with peace, mercy, and justice, with hope, faith, and love. Perhaps that is the only way the world and the words truly connect. Integrity is a way to beat our swords into ploughshares, and our spears into pruning hooks. These last are not sky hooks. They are real hooks, with real goodness attached. We need to heed the true authority of words united to the worth of the person.

Bibliography

Adams, Marilyn McCord. "Sin as Uncleanness." In *Philosophical Perspectives*, vol. 5, *Philosophy of Religion*, edited by James E. Tomberlin, 1–27. Atascadero, CA: Ridgeview, 1992.
———. "Theodicy without Blame." *Philosophical Topics* 16 (1988) 215–45.
Athanasius. *On the Incarnation*. Translated and edited by a religious of CSMV. Crestwood, NY: St. Vladimir's Seminary Press, 1944.
Atwood, Margaret. *Cat's Eye*. New York: Doubleday, 1988.
Augustine. *The Confessions of St. Augustine*. Translated by John K. Ryan. New York: Image, 1966,
Austin, J. L. "Ifs and Cans." *Proceedings of the British Academy* (1956).
Barfield, Owen. *Saving the Appearances: A Study in Idolatry*. 2nd ed. Hanover, NH: Wesleyan University Press, 1988.
Berry, Wendell. "Christianity and the Survival of Creation." In *Sex, Economy, Freedom and Community*, 93–116. New York: Pantheon, 1994.
———. *The Hidden Wound*. San Francisco: North Point, 1989.
———. "Standing by Words". In *Standing by Words*, 24–63. San Francisco: North Point, 1983.
Bilezikian, Gilbert. *Beyond Sex Roles: What the Bible Says about a Woman's Place in Church and Family*. Grand Rapids: Baker, 1985.
Bloom, Anthony. *Beginning to Pray*. New York: Paulist, 1970.
Chesterton, G. K. *Orthodoxy*. Garden City, NY: Image, 1959.
Eco, Umberto. *The Name of the Rose*. Translated by William Weaver. San Diego: Harcourt, 1983.
———. *Six Walks in the Fictional Woods*. The Charles Eliot Norton Lectures 1993. Cambridge, MA: Harvard University Press, 1994.
Gill, Eric. "First Things." In *A Holy Tradition of Working*. West Stockbridge, MA: Lindisfarne, 1983
Hallie, Phillip. "From Cruelty to Goodness." In *Vice and Virtue in Everyday Life*, edited by Christina Sommers and Fred Sommers, 5–20. New York: Harcourt, 1985.
Howard, Thomas. *On Being Catholic*. New York: Ignatius, 1997.
Jaspers, Karl. *Philosophy of Existence*. Translated by Richard F. Grabau. Philadelphia: University of Pennsylvania Press, 1971.
Langland, William. *Piers Ploughman*. Reprinted in *Working in America: A Humanities Reader*, edited by Robert Sessions and Jack Wortman. Notre Dame: University of Notre Dame Press, 1992.

Bibliography

Marcel, Gabriel. *The Philosophy of Existentialism*. Translated by Manya Harari. New York: Citadel, 1984.

McLeod-Harrison, Mark. *Make/believing the World(s): Toward a Christian Ontological Pluralism*. Montreal: McGill-Queens University Press, 2009.

———. *Repairing Eden: Mysticism, Humility and the Existential Problem of Religious Diversity*. Montreal: McGill-Queens University Press, 2005.

McLeod-Harrison, Susan. *Saving Women from the Church: How Jesus Mends a Divide*. Newberg, OR: Barclay, 2008.

Nozick, Robert. *The Examined Life: Philosophical Meditations*. New York: Simon & Schuster, 1989

Pascal, Blaise. *Pensées and Other Writings*. Translated by Honor Levi. Oxford: Oxford University Press, 2008.

Percy, Walker. "Naming and Being." *The Personalist* 41 (1960) 148–57.

Plantinga, Alvin. *God, Freedom and Evil*. Grand Rapids: Eerdmans, 1977.

Plato. *Phaedo*. In *Five Dialogues*, translated by G. M. Grube. Indianapolis: Hackett, 2002.

Sartre, Jean Paul. "Existentialism is Humanism." Reprinted as "The Humanism of Existentialism." In *Essays in Existentialism*. New York: Citadel, 1993.

———. *Nausea*. Translated by Lloyd Alexander. Norfolk, CT: New Directions, 1964.

Sayers, Dorothy. *The Mind of the Maker*. San Francisco: Harper & Row, 1979.

Stump, Eleanor. "Orthodoxy and Heresy." *Faith and Philosophy* 16:2 (1999) 147–63.

Thoreau, Henry David. *Walden*. New York: Harper, 1958.

Wangerin, Walter. "A Quiet Chamber Kept for Thee." In *The Manger Is Empty: Stories in Time*. San Francisco: Harper & Row, 1989.

www.ingramcontent.com/pod-product-compliance
Lightning Source LLC
Chambersburg PA
CBHW022119160426
43197CB00009B/1092